10 secrets to enjoying motherhood

the happiest
mom

Meagan Francis
and the editors of *Parenting* magazine

parenting
magazine

Happiness is within reach

Am I happy that I had kids? Of course! I love them even more than Mallomars and Orlando Bloom combined (though whoa, there's a mental image!). But have I become happier since I had kids? Hmm, that one's tougher. Maybe you feel the same way I do: My children bring me immense joy, no doubt about it. But the headaches of motherhood itself—broken shoelaces, crustless sandwiches, hours spent comforting my six-year-old daughter, who's sobbing because her big sister told her we all have skeletons inside us—can make happiness seem like a shiny golden apple at the top of a tall tree: always beckoning but maddeningly out of reach.

That's why, when I met Meagan, I immediately knew she was unique: a mother of five who's actually become happier as her family, and the frenzy, has grown. And as we at *Parenting* set out to bring this book to life with her, we quickly saw that what Meagan was creating was equally special—the next step in the evolution of parenting lit. Our mothers and grandmothers didn't have much to go on in terms of parenting books, and what little there was out there was bossy. From potty training to tantrum taming, there was a single right way to do everything. If you followed the rules, life would be perfect and your kids would be, too. If not, you'd raise brats and get scorned by society in the bargain. (Remember when moms who breastfed were called freaks? And then, later, when those who didn't nurse got called freaks? Freaky.)

So maybe it's no surprise that the pendulum has swung in the opposite direction in the past decade: moms coming out of the woodwork to write about the ugly underside of child rearing. Their tales are often pee-in-your-pants hilarious, and the underlying message that "being a mom is horribly hard, good thing we're all in it together" has helped many moms feel less isolated. On the other hand, making motherhood out to be one long, sleepless self-sacrifice ritual gets, well, tired after a while. Come on: Is the experience of raising kids that endlessly awful? If so, wouldn't the human race have died out by now?

What you're holding in your hands is a leap forward for all momkind—a true voice of reason. Meagan knows that the truth about motherhood lies somewhere in the middle of

You're going to make mistakes. The only unforgivable one is failing to forgive yourself for them.

all the extremes, and that's where this book takes us. Along the way, we also hear from moms in the Parenting.com community who share their in-the-trenches take on happier motherhood. Here at *Parenting*, we've never believed you have to be a perfect mom to be pretty happy, and that's how Meagan sees it, too, which is what made this a wonderful partnership. Yes, you're going to make mistakes, but the only unforgivable one is failing to forgive yourself for them.

Motherhood can be tough for sure, but it's also amazingly special. And, if you're curious about what Meagan's biggest secret to happiness is, I'll give it away right here: It's keeping that sentiment in mind, while using some surprisingly simple tricks to free yourself from needless worry and frustration. We're about to show you how. Think of each step as a rung on a ladder—leaned up against that tall apple tree. A sweeter life is within your reach! Read on, and above all, *savor*.

Deborah Skolnik
Senior Editor, *Parenting*

Happy moms raise happier kids

Moms are great at keeping an ear to the ground and an eye on the horizon for epidemics, whether an outbreak of lice at school or an especially nasty flu bug that's targeting every kid in the neighborhood. Meanwhile, though, many moms are suffering through their own epidemic and not even fully realizing it: rampant unhappiness.

Did you know that, on average, parents are 7 percent less content than their childless peers? Many parents report that they feel happier grocery shopping than hanging out with their children! Since my book, *Raising Happiness: 10 Simple Steps for More Joyful Kids and Happier Parents*, came out, I've met so many unhappy mothers that I've come to the conclusion that there are a lot of moms out there who really love their kids, but don't really love their lives.

This isn't the way parenting is supposed to be! It's true, our lives are busier than ever, and there's never been more pressure to produce outstanding kids (even while often coping with demanding jobs, financial pressures, and massive time crunches). The good news is that there are simple strategies that can make your days more relaxed and rewarding—kids, commitments, and all.

Here's why: Happiness is better thought of as a skill—or a set of skills—than it is an inborn personality trait. Think of building your happiness the way you would if you wanted to become more fluent in a foreign language: Find a good teacher and an engaging text, and practice practice practice.

You've found a great teacher in Meagan. Chapter by chapter, she makes every lesson lighthearted and fun. You'll learn how to take small but significant steps toward happiness, like lightening up (so what if your kid went to school in dirty socks!), tidying up (just enough to save your sanity), and ditching whatever drags you down (homemade Chinese yo-yo party favors, anyone?).

Think boosting your happiness is selfish? That focusing on yourself will take too much time and attention—time and attention that's better spent on your kids? Short-circuit the guilt trip. Instead, try to look at it this way: One very good reason for you to focus on your own happiness is actually for your kids' sake. Honest.

For starters, when we moms do what it takes to be happy ourselves, our children mimic us, making it more likely that they will be happier both as children and adults. If we model

Your happiness can be delightfully contagious, and your kids are often the first to catch it.

happiness—and all the skills that go with it—our kids are likely to behave in the same way. Your happiness can be delightfully contagious, and your kids are often the first to catch it. Before they're even a week old, in fact, children start mirroring their parents' emotions—it's one of the key ways they learn about feelings. And because research shows that people's emotions tend to converge—that is to say, we become more similar emotionally the more we hang out together—it follows that the happier we parents are, the happier our children are ultimately bound to be.

Unfortunately, our kids pick up on our less positive emotions, too. There are degrees of unhappiness, ranging from everyday angst to clinical depression, a treatable medical condition. In fact, as many as one out of five women will suffer from some form of depression during her life, frequently during the prime parenting years of ages 25 to 44, with pregnancy and postpartum being especially vulnerable times.

If you are persistently sad or anxious, seek help, for both your sake and your family's. Mothers who suffer from untreated depression tend to be less sensitive to children's needs and less able to correct negative behaviors or play with kids in ways that spur emotional growth. Studies have shown that anxiety, too, can rub off on children—nervous mothers are at risk for having children who exhibit similar high-strung tendencies.

But the good news is that taking steps toward being a happier person will make you a better mother. Positive emotions help us become better listeners and more creative problem solvers. In turn, we feel warmer toward our children and are much more responsive to them.

In fact, happiness will make you better at a lot of things. On average, happy people are more successful than unhappy ones at both work and love. They get better performance reviews, have more prestigious jobs, and earn higher salaries. They are more likely to tie the knot, and, once they do, they are more satisfied with their marriages.

Happy people also tend to be healthier and live longer. In her groundbreaking research on positivity, psychologist Barbara Fredrickson has found that positive emotions:

• Broaden our thinking in ways that make us more flexible, more able to see the big picture, and more creative.

• Accumulate and compound over time, transforming us for the better by building the resources—strength, wisdom, friendship, and resilience—we need to truly thrive.

• Are the most important ingredient in determining a person's resilience in hard times. Positive emotions help our bodies and our minds cope with stress, challenges, and negative feelings.

Here's the takeaway: If you make yourself an example of happiness in action, and model the skills to achieve it, your kids are bound to pick up the knack for crafting a life with a positive flow and feel.

Meanwhile, you will be reaping all the benefits of looking on the bright side, too. Being happy right now—not after the kids are grown and the mortgage paid, or once the PTA fundraiser

> **Being happy right now—not after the kids are grown and the mortgage paid—is no small thing.**

is finally over, or when you've mastered the art of getting three kids packed for school and getting your own teeth brushed—is no small thing. It won't be enough to look back decades from today and think that everything was worth it because you raised great kids; you deserve to have a great time raising them. Read on for some great tips from Meagan about how to do this.

Enjoy becoming happier!

Christine Carter, PhD
Author of *Raising Happiness: 10 Simple Steps for More Joyful Kids and Happier Parents*

1

take the easy way out

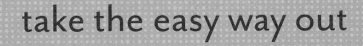

Are you a happy mom? Do you believe you can use the words "happy" and "mom" in the same sentence? Do you believe you can use the word "happy" at all, without it being followed by "birthday," a piñata, and an extensive cleanup? Do you want to be a happier mom? Who doesn't, right?

Being a parent these days doesn't always look so rosy—if you read all the confessional mommy blogs and memoirs out there that dish the real poop (literally!). You hear motherhood talked about in terms of surviving and coping—not being happy or having fun, unless a margarita is involved. I get it: Having a baby and raising children are life-changing experiences. Motherhood is challenging. It's frustrating. It's exhausting. Sometimes it makes you want to curl up into the fetal position and call for your own mommy.

But while motherhood isn't a 24/7 ride on the fun-o-matic, neither is it a 24/7 ride in a Cheerios-strewn minivan. We can learn to deal with the hard stuff, let go of what doesn't matter, and enjoy our lives as mothers. Yes, we really can all be happy moms. And I hope this book helps you become one.

I wasn't always the happiest mom on the block. When my two oldest kids were young, I fantasized about running away from the zoo our home had become and joining the circus instead, or the coast guard—really, any group who'd have me. Everything seemed so hard, and every decision weighed heavy on my mind: What if I made the wrong choice? But as my husband and I added more children to the mix (five in all), something surprising happened. Instead of becoming more unhappy, stressed, and anxious, I became happier, more relaxed, and more confident. Through trial and error, and the natural ups and downs of raising a growing family, I've figured out some strategies—some obvious, some unexpected—that help keep my scale tipped toward the "happy" mark.

In this book, I'll explain what I've learned. I'll also share lessons from the editors of *Parenting* magazine and insights from its readers. I've organized this advice into ten secrets, and the first one I want to talk about, the one I think is the basis of all the others, is this: *It's okay to take the easy way out.*

It's true that being a happy mom sometimes means doing things the hard way. Maybe we cook from scratch because we enjoy it. Other times, we choose the harder road instead of the path of least resistance because it'll make things easier in the long run—like teaching our kids to tie their laces so we don't have to do it for them five times a day once we can no longer find Velcro-tab shoes in their size.

Whether it's sewing your kids' clothes or building your own picnic table, if anything you're doing "the hard way" brings you satisfaction and joy, or you feel is so much better for your family, then I'm not going to quibble with you. You're talking to

While motherhood isn't a 24/7 ride on the fun-o-matic, neither is it a 24/7 ride in a Cheerios-strewn minivan.

the woman who actually enjoyed laundering and folding cloth diapers. Hey, it made me happy!

But we all probably have things we pour our energy into without having a good reason why. Are there a few things in your life that seem harder than they should be? If you've found yourself packing your child a lunch worthy of a four-star restaurant when she'd be happy with PBJ, or if you keep dragging your toddler to that over-crowded story time at the library even though you'd both rather settle in with a book on your bed, those activities may be worth reconsidering.

I admit it: There have been times that I've done things a certain way to make a good impression on other moms (or at the very least, to avoid looking like a loser). Like the time I made healthy sugar-free cookies for playgroup rather than bringing along the usual Goldfish crackers. I could much more easily have brought a big bunch of bananas—it would have been equally healthy and not as time-consuming!

Remember that because it's technically possible for us to pull off something ("something" being anything from clipping your newborn's micro-nails to helping your daughter make a volcano for science class using toothpicks, fruit leather, soda,

Any time something feels hard every time, ask whether it could be any easier with a little thought.

and Mentos) doesn't mean that we should. It's part of that supermom myth that I'd like to throw in the Diaper Genie.

Are you sensing a pattern? Any time something feels hard every time you do it, ask whether it could be any easier with a little thought. When we look closely at our motivations and weed out those energy-suckers, we can focus on the things that really matter to us and forget the rest.

Let's take a look at some of the not-so-great reasons moms sometimes sweat it out by ourselves—take the quiz on page 16 to identify any that slow you down—and why it's okay to choose the less-taxing route. Then read the previews of the coming chapters, so you can think about which will be the most helpful for you.

What matters to moms?

No one knows the answer to this question better than *Parenting* magazine, which has assembled a special nationwide group of mothers—from first-timers to vets, singles to happily-marrieds—to sound off on a variety of issues. Dubbed the MomConnection, this panel had plenty to say when *Parenting* conducted a Mood of Moms study and asked them what makes them smile.

More than 1,000 moms in all responded, dishing on how satisfied (or not!) they are with more than 60 factors—from relationships to money. The results? The top five factors that make the biggest difference to our happiness are:

- A strong relationship with our partner (or, for single moms, a satisfying love life)

- A positive outlook for the future

- Believing that we're raising happy kids

- Feeling appreciated for the hard work we do at home and at work

- A strong and supportive network of family and friends

Q/A

What motivates you, Mama?

What ties you up? What drags you down? Take our quiz and discover your first step to freedom!

1 *During your most frustrating parenting moments, how do you tend to feel?*
   a. Uncertain. You want to make the right choices but aren't sure what they are.
   b. Tired. Kids are a lot of work, and your standards are high.
   c. Overwhelmed. You can't keep up, much less get ahead.
   d. Angry. No one seems to care about what you want.
   e. Lonely. There's no one to share the load.

2 *Which of these mothering crises is likely to strike at your house?*
   a. Your three-year-old doesn't seem ready for potty training, but her daycare provider is putting on the pressure.
   b. It's midnight the night before your fourth-grade daughter's recital, and you're sewing sequins on her costume. (What's a little mermaid without a sparkly tail?)
   c. Your daughter needs her birth certificate so she can enroll in summer camp. Today. And you have no idea where to find it—or the camp registration form, for that matter.
   d. You're supposed to go out with some friends (so rare!), but your son reminded you that he has a karate class.
   e. Your infant has a high fever and is screaming nonstop. He needs to get to after-hours urgent care ASAP, but you have no one you can ask to watch your preschooler.

3 *Which of the following phrases are you most likely to say?*
   a. "I don't know. What do you think?"
   b. "But I need to do this!"
   c. "Oh no, I forgot!"
   d. "I guess I'll change my plans."
   e. Since you don't have anyone to talk to except your kids, it probably has something to do with the potty.

4 *How would you describe date nights?*
   a. Anxious. Did you choose the right babysitter? Are your kids even old enough to be left with a sitter?
   b. Distracted. You talk about the kids and work, but you can't get those dirty dishes in the sink out of your mind.
   c. Cancelled. You totally forgot about the parent-teacher conference you had scheduled. Whoops!
   d. Rare. There's always so much to do for the kids, you don't have much time for the two of you.
   e. Precious. They're fun! And date nights are the only time you eat with someone who doesn't need you to wipe his mouth (well, maybe sometimes).

5 *What is your biggest obstacle when it comes to doing things you love, like pursuing a hobby or reading a book?*
   a. You spend what little free time you have reading up on the next stage of parenting—that's the priority right now.
   b. Trying to keep the house in shape and managing your kids' schedules takes up all your time.
   c. Free time catches you off guard, so you spend most of it looking for what you need to get the ball rolling, whether it's knitting needles or that book your friend lent you.
   d. If you have "free time," shouldn't you spend every minute of it with your kids?
   e. You'd love to see a movie or have a cup of coffee with someone, but you don't have anyone to ask.

Quiz key

Maybe your answers were all over the map, or mostly one letter. Most of us could probably learn something from each category, so let's take a peek at what your responses mean:

Mostly A's: Insecurity could be holding you back. At some point, with kids, you have to trust your gut and take a leap.

Mostly B's: Whoa, take it easy! Parenting isn't meant to be a competitive sport. (Shopping, on the other hand . . .)

Mostly C's: Some simple order could reduce the chaos in your life. How can you find happiness if you can't find your keys?

Mostly D's: You've moved your needs off the back burner and into the freezer. Oh yeah, they're in there somewhere—check behind the mystery meat.

Mostly E's: You need support—people who can cover your back and help share the work of raising kids.

No matter what you answered on the quiz, this book is packed with been-there anecdotes and tips to help you. Here's a chapter-by-chapter preview:

Aim low, and go slow

In chapter 2, we'll talk all about adjusting expectations—of ourselves, our kids, our spouses, and the rest of the world. Do you have sky-high expectations for yourself or feel pressured by other people's? Either way, you would probably let out a sigh of relief if you cut yourself some slack from time to time. I'm not recommending that you completely give up your standards, but by embracing a slower pace and setting realistic goals, you'll cultivate more happiness for the whole family.

Trust your gut

I've taken to heart what too many parenting "experts" have said, even when their advice didn't line up with my instincts. For example, one popular parenting manual suggests feeding a newborn baby only every four hours, no matter how hard he cries, how hungry he seems, or how uncomfortable Mom gets. I tried this method once, but by the time we got to hour three, my baby was hysterical, I was in tears, and I was so engorged that I made Heidi Montag look like an 11-year-old boy.

Some "expert" advice borders on the ridiculous. Once, a psychologist told me during a magazine article interview that parents should train a bird to hop in front of non-crawling babies to tempt them to pick up those knees and get moving. (I suspect he was raised by cuckoos.) Nobody knows your child better than you. In chapter 3, I'll lay out a strategy for becoming your own parenting guru so you feel confident making decisions without second-guessing.

Keep it real

You're a different person than you were before you became a parent, but you're still you. Chapter 4 asks you to recognize and embrace the positive changes that go along with your new role and celebrates how being a mom makes you even more wonderful. Having a child offers chances to try new things and, who knows, you might like them! It's easy, though, to fall into the trap of comparing yourself to other moms. News flash: Some moms love to coach softball, bake pies, or dig worms for a fishing trip—not all moms do. Maybe, instead, you're the mom who tells the best jokes or is always up for a snuggle (and, admit it, a bowl of Cheez Doodles) on the sofa.

Find your tribe

Sometimes we moms think we should be able to manage our lives all by ourselves, or feel like we have to. We may resist asking for a hand or feel like we don't have even one minute to ask for help. Maybe we don't have anyone to call since our

"I bathe my son and daughter together, microwave frozen veggies, and sometimes have the kids sleep in their clothes. Once or twice a month, I announce it's 'mix-up night' and serve cereal and frozen waffles for dinner. The kids love it, but I feel guilty. But I'd rather feel guilty than more stressed!" -Debbie

friends are equally busy and we don't have family nearby. It's no coincidence that my least-happy periods of motherhood have also been the loneliest. But it's one thing to know you need friends and another thing entirely to start building that fabled village. Making friends with other moms isn't always as easy as dropping in on a neighbor for a cup of coffee. (Bringing low-fat blueberry muffins that actually taste good, though, will up your chances of success.) In chapter 5, we'll talk about easy ways to get support and camaraderie, plus some grown-up playdates on your calendar.

Go with the flow

If you have every detail of every day mapped out, you're not leaving much room for dealing with last-minute emergencies or simply changing your mind. Flying by the seat of your pants doesn't always end well either. But funny enough, some planning can help you prepare for and cope with change. Chapter 6 is about balancing organization with flexibility and fostering your ability to go with the flow.

Make your bed

If every day is a whirlwind of soccer cleats gone astray, missing permission slips, pre-dinner chaos (and where'd that hamster go?), it'll be hard to find enough mojo to enjoy a walk around the block with your kids. The trick is to identify the triggers that make you crazy—stacks of unread newspapers or toothpaste on the sink. In chapter 7, we'll talk about how addressing the crazy-makers that really bug you can give your happiness a boost.

Have a plan

Are you a "big idea" person but maybe not as spot on when it comes to details? Or do you reliably tie up the loose ends but tend to forget to step back and look at the whole picture? Or does it depend on the context, for instance, work vs. home? All parents have to wing it at times, but it helps to have a general idea of where you're headed, so you're parenting with purpose, not panic. Busy moms also need time-management skills so that

Five ways to say "no"

From chaperoning prom to selling wrapping paper as a fundraiser, moms receive a lot of requests for help. If you're on the spot and feel uncomfortable saying, "I'm sorry, I'm unavailable," here are five other ways to say "no" gracefully:

1   The "not that, but this" maneuver: "Sorry, I won't be able to cover for your babysitter all week, but I'd be happy to watch Jacob on Tuesday."

2   The "blame someone else" technique: "I'd love to run the concession stand for the football game on Thursday, but my husband has a class that night."

3   The "let me think it over" method: "Going on the field trip sounds fun, but I'd have to figure out childcare for the baby. Can I get back to you?"

4   The "my strengths lie elsewhere" tactic: "You know, I'm not the right person to solicit donations for the school's silent auction. I'd do a better job designing the flyer."

5   The "don't promise, but leave the door open" approach: "I don't think I can help, but I will if I can." Later, any help (even a little bit) from you will be a delightful surprise!

their best-laid plans don't melt like yesterday's Popsicle. Chapter 8 will help you find an everyday rhythm that makes the most of your time and a planning system that works for you. Checking one thing off the list is a surefire way to up your happiness quotient—think of how satisfying it is to accomplish what

Being a happy mom is all about being yourself, not what anyone else thinks you should be.

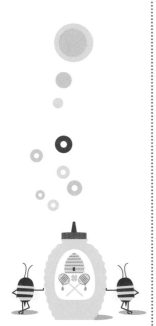

you planned. Planning can also prevent last-minute crises and make it easier to stay calm in the face of life's surprises.

Look out for #1

There's no crime in being a little bit selfish. Even the simplest things can start to feel like a chore if you're drawing from an empty well. You're still a person, with needs (think adequate sleep) and wants (think George Clooney—hey, we said "wants," not "gonna-gets"). It's as important to take time and energy for your own health and well-being as for your family's.

Do you pick at your child's leftover mac and cheese instead of fixing yourself a decent lunch? Is your only source of exercise picking your toddler up—and putting her down, and picking her up, and putting her down . . . ? When was the last time you read a book that didn't rhyme? Chapter 9 gives permission to pay attention to yourself and ideas for finding time to do it.

I encourage you to pay attention to your health, including your mental health. I hope this book will help every reader become a happier mom. However, if you feel persistently sad or anxious, or your gut tells you the way you feel just isn't right, please touch base with your doctor.

Signs of depression, for instance, vary. One person might feel irritable, while another has trouble concentrating. Postpartum depression reveals itself in its own ways, like feeling a lack of bonding with your baby. Research shows that receiving treatment positively affects the way a mom struggling with depression interacts with her child, so keep in mind that seeking help matters for your family's well-being, too.

Love your love life

Parenting's MomConnection panel ranked their love lives as the most important factor in how happy they are as moms (see page 15). No wonder. If you have a strong partnership, you'll have someone in your corner to back up your discipline decisions, to laugh with when your preschooler accidentally swears, or simply to kick your feet up with before you both start snoring. Chapter 10 discusses nurturing that relationship so you stay on the same page as parents and partners. And if you're a single mom, at some point you'll want your love life to take center stage again, if it hasn't already.

What matters to you

If you're like me, I'm guessing you recognized some areas where you could use a little help turning up the happy. I know you've got a lot on your plate. Read the chapters in any order, and feel free to read the ones that speak most strongly to you first and dive back in more deeply later.

Being a happy mom is all about being yourself, not what anyone else thinks you should be, and relaxing enough to enjoy your kids and the rest of your life without too much second-guessing. Throughout the book, I offer ideas that I hope will inspire you to move past the "shoulds" and guilt, and be the kind of mother you want to be.

Step by step, we'll help you distinguish between what really matters to you and what doesn't make the cut. We'll create a plan for helping you muster up the self-confidence to say "no" and the courage to say "yes" based on what you want to do. And along the way, you'll figure out how to go from "It's all so hard" to "You know what? I'm pretty happy."

(easy jump start)

Setting a password for an online shopping account or the new computer system at work? Reference an inside joke or pick something else that will make you happy every time you type it, like MonkeyToes123 (don't ask!). Every time you log on, you'll have a reason to smile.

2

aim low, and go slow

My oldest son, Jacob, was an easy baby and an even easier toddler. "Look at *that* kid," I'd whisper to my husband, pointing out someone else's screaming child in a restaurant while our little angel sat quietly. Naturally, I assumed Jacob's behavior reflected our superior parenting skills.

Then our second son, Isaac, stormed into our lives. He was always either howling in anger or shrieking in joy. Once he was mobile, we could barely leave the house. Climbing, throwing, trying to run into traffic—he was up for any of it. (And I was up for that last one myself, after long days with him.)

I wondered how I'd screwed up this time around. Or worse, was there something wrong with Isaac? Was it really too much to expect a toddler to sit in a restaurant high chair and munch saltines while we ate dinner? Yep.

We moms tend to have a lot of expectations. Then, when things don't pan out, we often take the fall.

After comparing notes with a few moms, I found out that Isaac's behavior was appropriate for his age. I'd been fooled by Jacob's easy-going nature, but Isaac was closer to the norm. Chances are good that you've had a similar fantasy-meet-reality moment. We moms tend to have a lot of expectations: of our kids, our spouses, other moms, and, perhaps most potentially damaging of all, of ourselves. When things don't pan out, we often take the fall—whether it's our fault or not.

Maybe you always assumed you'd serve on the PTA and, instead, you're so busy you didn't even remember to sign off on your first-grader's progress report in time. Did you ever set out to make your child a homemade birthday cake shaped like a carousel—even though you've only made brownies from a mix since your Easy-Bake oven days—and then felt crushed when it came out looking more like a maximum-security prison? Have you ever thought if you tried a little harder, you could get it all together?

If so, you might want to rethink your approach. "Aim low, and go slow" is secret number two of happier motherhood. It's all about setting reasonable expectations—for you and everyone around you—and being patient with yourself and others. That way, you might end up pleasantly surprised by a perfect day rather than unpleasantly surprised by a normal one.

Set your own standards

How low is low enough? Are we talking preprinted address labels or a family of dust bunnies living under the table? It can vary from one situation (and mom) to the next. One way to tell whether you're cutting yourself, your kids, or your spouse enough slack is to consider how you react when things don't go according to plan. What you do when things go awry typically reflects how realistic your expectations are.

Some mistakes are a Big Deal—say your nanny doesn't buckle your baby in her car seat—and warrant a big reaction. But that kind of snafu is pretty rare. Most of the time, we could stand to scale back our expectations of ourselves and others. Instead of aiming for perfection (a spotless house, cooked-from-scratch meals, and squeaky-clean kids) and feeling disappointed when we miss the mark, by aiming low (a house that's not condemned by the health board, box-o-noodles with frozen peas on the side, and kids who can remember their last bath), we'll pretty much always exceed our goals. Take the quiz on page 28 to learn more about how high you set the bar.

"As for trying to be a domestic goddess—give it up, sister! I am a bit of a control freak, and I wanted things to be perfect when my son came into the world. Then I realized that as long as I work 40 or more hours a week and want to spend time with my husband and son when I am at home, sometimes other things are going to fall through the cracks."
-HappyMother

Q/A

Come on, what do you expect?

When something gets screwed up, what do you do? Take this quiz to see what your reactions say about your expectations.

1 *You pick up your son from daycare. As you're putting his boots on, you notice his socks are inside out and, oops, it appears they aren't even clean. You:*

   a. Brush it off as a minor wardrobe malfunction. At least he wore two socks.

   b. Grit your teeth. Wasn't your husband supposed to help him get dressed this morning?

   c. Convince yourself that your child's caregiver thinks you have the IQ of a handful of stale Cheerios (which, incidentally, you found in the bottom of your purse).

   d. Look over your shoulder. Did any of the other moms see?

2 *You take your daughter to her first dentist visit and learn that she already has two cavities. You:*

   a. Are surprised—but feel better when the dentist reassures you that some kids are more susceptible to tooth decay and says she'll keep a close eye on your daughter's teeth.

   b. Write a mental thank-you note to your mother-in-law for all the caramels and lollipops she's been slipping your kids. It's a miracle they have any teeth at all!

   c. Are embarrassed. The dentist must think you're bending the truth about how often she brushes.

   d. Wonder what you'll say when a friend brags that her child has never had a cavity.

3 *You notice an invitation addressed to your son in a stack of papers. The birthday party's tomorrow; the reply-by date was five days ago. So you:*

   a. Call and see if it's still possible for your child to come party down. After all, you would understand if another parent were in the same situation.

b. Tell your son he should have shown you the invitation sooner. Gosh, kid, do the words *"répondez s'il vous plaît"* mean nothing to you?

c. Call and apologize profusely, begging forgiveness for being so rude.

d. Ignore it and hope no one asks.

Quiz key

Mostly A's: Realist You know things frequently don't go according to plan and that most mishaps aren't worth getting bent out of shape over.

Mostly B's: Blamer When plans go awry, your knee-jerk reaction is to lash out at someone: your spouse, your child, that candy-pushin' granny.

Mostly C's: "My Bad!" Martyr A perfectionist, you feel like you failed when even small things don't go the way you planned.

Mostly D's: Queen of Denial You're afraid of other moms noticing your missteps. You'd prefer to ignore it when something is amiss and hope no one else notices. Say, you might be looking at a bright future in politics.

"I had a no-TV-ever goal. That was ridiculous! I realized I'm not a bad parent if my daughter watches a bit of TV. She learns from discussing the things the characters do, and it's easier to cook or do other chores when she's watching a show. As long as I monitor what she watches and for how long, and am available to interact and talk with her about what she sees, I feel comfortable."
-DJonesz

Did you learn anything surprising from your quiz results? Maybe it never occurred to you that your tendency to always pin the blame on yourself—or pass the buck—means you're expecting too much. After all, you wouldn't feel the need to point so many fingers if you didn't feel let down so often.

Of course, we all have our areas where we have a hard time relaxing our standards. For example, maybe you have no problem buying ready-made costumes (the day before Halloween, natch) but can't let go of the idea that your house should stay neat once you've picked up (as your sixth-grade daughter and her friends decide to have a pillow fight for the 189th time today). Or perhaps you take your preschooler's bed-wetting relapse in stride but tense up when he hits the mooning-strangers-at-the-supermarket phase. (What, just us?)

No one can be perfectly realistic at all times—there's a bit of the Blamer, Martyr, and Queen of Denial (see quiz key on previous page) lurking in all of us. Here are some suggestions for taking a closer look at your standards and giving everyone around you—including yourself!—a break.

Pause the blame game

Are you like me? I try to run my family's life like a well-oiled machine (even if we do have a few screws loose), and when a part breaks, it's hard for me to accept that it could be my fault. Like the time I forgot my son had morning tennis camp until the last minute and had to drive to drop him off in my pajamas, with Bride of Frankenstein bed hair and raging morning breath, praying the whole time I wouldn't get pulled over by a good-looking cop. Worse, when I got home, I called my husband and blamed him for not putting the camp dates on the calendar.

Thing is, it wasn't a big enough deal to get upset about. And putting the dates on the calendar—which I hadn't checked the night before anyway—wasn't necessarily his job to begin with. A few minutes after slamming down the phone, I called back and apologized. By blaming him, I'd wasted 15 minutes stewing and hadn't fixed the problem—that we both needed to do a better job keeping track of the kids' activities and divvying up tasks. We also need to give ourselves a break when someone is running late or overlooks something. When I stopped "feeding" my anger by chewing out my husband, I realized that there are worse fates than facing down a handsome policeman—say, having to sit in said policeman's car due to forgetting my driver's license. Not that I would know.

Most moms are like you: doing their best to raise their kids.

As a recovering blamer, I still feel the urge to point fingers, but instead I try to calm myself down by taking a deep breath and asking these questions:

• Am I feeling guilty and trying to deflect responsibility away from myself?
• Are my expectations too high for my children's stage of development?
• Does it matter? Is it even worth giving another thought?
• Will I remember this in a day, a week, a year?
• If I made the mistake, how would I want to be treated?
• Am I copying the way I was raised? Is it right for my kids?
• Am I taking my child's perspective into account?

Don't worry about being judged

If you feel like every mom at playgroup is whispering behind her hand because your kid took a swing at another child, try to keep in mind that most moms are like you: doing their best to raise their kids. So what if you've never heard the mom with the perfect hair in the impeccably clean car ever raise her voice to her three adorable children? She could have a stack of Twinkies hidden under the seat that she uses to bribe them into good behavior, and her own perma-sugar rush would explain her annoyingly good mood too. You can never really know what goes on in someone else's life! (How many times have you been shocked to hear that friends—who you thought were a perfect match—are divorcing?)

Why not try being honest with other moms about your mothering meltdowns? Playground and watercooler confessions can be the kind of bonding experience that sparks new friendships. Try airing some of your dirty laundry to another mom (like, for instance, that dirty laundry is exactly what your kid's wearing, because he's refused to put on anything except his Pokémon shirt since Monday). See what happens—maybe she'll dish some dirt in return.

Also try showing other moms compassion when they mess up. As tempting as it can be to join the mommy wars on Facebook and blogs (better than *The Real Housewives of New Jersey* at times), try to avoid getting sucked in. The more you read and hear other people criticizing moms in general, the more judged and defensive you're likely to feel. But if you extend grace and understanding to moms, you'll start to recognize that we can be imperfect and awesome at the same time. A knowing smile

A knowing smile is sometimes all it takes to help another mom feel understood.

is sometimes all it takes to help another mom feel understood. She'll likely grant you the same favor next time it's your little one who rips off her diaper and puts it on her head at the park.

Cultivate confidence

Aiming low is different from giving up. It doesn't mean you stop reading to your second-grader altogether because you don't have time to do it every night, or let your five-year-old turn into the playground terrorist because he's going through a "difficult" stage. Instead, maybe you read to your daughter on

Make don't-do lists

Most of us are good at making to-do lists. But what about the things we'd like to do some day, but the timing isn't ideal now? Give yourself permission to put them on the back burner by making a "don't do now" list. That way, you remove them from today's already full to-do list—and you know they won't be forgotten either.

A "don't do now" list might include:

1 Run a marathon, take a Zumba class, practice yoga, or swing dance.

2 Host dinner parties. Fun when you have lots of time to cook and chat. Not so fun when you're trying to rock a baby and roll pasta dough simultaneously.

3 Knit, needlepoint, crochet, sew, quilt, embroider—or anything that requires a needle.

4 Make scrapbooks.

5 Write a book.

And then there are the things that we don't want to do now—or ever—but think we should. It's okay to decide to put some things aside for eternity by adding them to a "don't do ever" list. Consciously making the decision to let yourself off the hook can lighten your mental and emotional load.

A "don't do ever" list might include:

1 Read newspapers more than one week old.

2 Buy clothes that can't go in the dryer or that need ironing. Enough said.

3 Sign up your child for more than one weekend class or team. I promise, your four-year-old will become a functional adult even if she never plays T-ball.

4 Make fundraising phone calls.

5 Write a book.

the weekends, when your schedule is a little more relaxed. And maybe you'll avoid the playground during peak hours, and give your son—and yourself—plenty of time to work through his temporary Gordon Ramsay phase. Set the bar low and don't rush yourself, and you'll succeed most of the time. And with every success, your confidence will grow.

But it's not always easy to know where to invest your energy and time—and what to let go of. That's where the three P's—priorities, perspective, and probabilities—come in.

Priorities

You're faced with an infinite number of things you could do for your child: Create a photo album detailing every waking moment of her life, take her to the park at the crack of dawn to nurture her budding interest in birds, set aside half your paycheck so she can spend her summer at violin camp (you're sure she's prodigy material). But here's one thing that's certain: You can't do it all, at least not well, and not right now.

You'll want to nurture your child's interests, but not at the expense of your sleep or savings account.

That scrapbook might get made, but it's okay if it takes so long that you've forgotten what's going on in half the pictures by the time you get around to sticking them onto the page. Photos are all digital now anyway!

Your child will have lots of interests in her life, and you'll want to nurture them, but not necessarily at the expense of your sleep or emergency savings account. The secret is figuring out what your current priorities are, so that you can focus on the stuff that coincides with them right now. Perhaps you're tutoring math in your child's classroom, soliciting donations for the PTA fundraising auction, and helping paint the sets for the school play. Oh, and there's that full-time job too.

You're spread as thin as a peanut-butter sandwich on grocery-shopping day, but what should you cut? Think about your top priorities. It could be something like this: I want to support my child's education, to use my creativity, and to have evenings free to spend with the family. Using this example, you may realize that tutoring has you away from the office more than you can afford, and asking for donations feels too far removed from your child. But you could happily paint sets on the weekends with your little Renoir (or maybe he's more of a Pollock). Then ditch the rest of it like yesterday's diapers—bowing out gracefully, of course (see page 21 for tips). Accepting that you can't handle it all allows you to focus on what you need and want to do.

Perspective

Sometimes I think fear causes us to compulsively set the bar too high. We might be afraid of what will happen if we don't live up to our own expectations, or if our kids don't live up to them. Often, though, we worry way more than the task at hand deserves. There have been nights when I woke up with my heart racing in anxiety because I realized that I forgot to turn on the dishwasher before I got in bed. To put even minor worries like this in perspective, I ask myself three things:

- What's the worst that could happen? My ten-year-old son might have to—gasp!—drink milk straight from the carton tomorrow morning. No child knows how to do that!
- Will this still trouble me far into the future? Ah, yes, The Great Dishwasher Disaster of March 7, 2011.
- Is there any possible upside to this oversight? Yes. My son might start to realize that dishes do not wash themselves.

It might seem silly to go through this exercise every single time you're stressing over something small, but after a while it became second nature to me. Consider trying this approach for a day and see what happens. Even if you fail to live up to your expectations a million times that day, I'm guessing that a little perspective will remind you that the results will rarely be tragic.

Probabilities (instead of possibilities)

Even after having five kids, I still dream of having Angelina Jolie's abs, getting discovered on *American Idol*, and renovating my crumbling 100-year-old Victorian to HGTV standards. It would also be fabulous if my husband could bring himself to sell his old Transformers (like I don't know they're in the closet), my kids got straight A's, and my four-year-old would outgrow his habit of slamming doors during the baby's nap. The optimistic side of me says that any of those things are possible. But my realistic side reminds me that none of them are very probable.

Even after having five kids, I still dream of having Angelina Jolie's abs. Sure, it's possible—but not probable.

Making a distinction between probable and possible helps shape more realistic expectations. Keep this in mind when you make a to-do list (see page 33 on creating don't-do lists). Aim for only a handful of tasks that are pretty easy to accomplish, as long as nobody in your house breaks a window while scaling the living-room wall using the curtains à la Spider-Man. These can be as simple as making spaghetti for dinner, helping your daughter with her spelling, and taking the trash out. Chances are good that you'll be able to tick off at least a couple of things on your low-aiming list—and you'll feel so victorious you might even manage to remember the recycling bin this time.

Hope for the best, prepare for the rest

I'm not suggesting that you ought to have no goals for yourself or your family. What mom doesn't hope that her children will behave reasonably well, grow up to be productive adults, and make her proud along the way? In fact, by letting your child take charge of himself, one step at a time, you're fostering his independence and taking things off of your own to-do list. So let him pour his own cereal (then spill it, then clean it up)— you'll probably add some happiness to both your lives!

It's a good idea to have achievable hopes and goals for ourselves too. (We'll talk more about planning in chapter 8.) But while we can plan for success and happiness, I guarantee that details will go awry every now and then. On the plus side, imperfect parenting gives our kids funny stories to tell later—like the time Mom got so flustered at discovering the three-year-old sporting a "haircut" from the eight-year-old barber that she had to put herself in time-out.

My standards for my kids' behavior are high, and yet, I can't expect that they will always meet them. I can hope my oldest son will wow the judges at the science fair and that all my boys will exhibit impeccable manners at church, but I'm far more likely to find that the "Mini Biodome" is an overturned Tupperware bowl with Fisher-Price Little People trapped inside, and I'll probably have to clamp a hand on a tiny mouth on Sunday morning to keep the whole congregation from hearing the announcement, "Mommy, I made a sneeze bubble!"

Reality check

I always tell people that going from my second to my third child was a much easier transition than going from one to two. By that time, I'd realized that the quickest path to mom happiness was not to expect too much of anyone. I had learned to target goals I know I can reach, to slow my day-to-day pace, and not to cry over spilled milk—or the juice that spilled right after I finished mopping up the milk.

The good news: You don't have to have multiple children to start adjusting your expectations. You can get going now, a little at a time. Avoid the office-supply store if your toddler is going through his klepto phase, nice though a free stapler would be. Dump the plans to make tomato bisque from scratch for Thanksgiving dinner (they don't call the canned kind mmm mmm good for nothing, you know). Forgive yourself for forgetting to take your book to book group—and to read it. Aim for *good enough*, and life will be better than ever.

(**easy jump start**)

Another school bake sale? Powdered sugar and colored sprinkles can add that homemade touch to store-bought baked goods, or you can offer to make signs or help set up the tables. You're still participating, but you won't spend hours baking grandma's Black Forest cake!

3

trust your gut

"Tummy *what?*" Moms on the playground lamented that their babies weren't getting enough of this mysterious thing called "tummy time" because they hated being placed facedown to play. My third son, William, was a few months old, and I'd never even heard of it.

I immediately went online to find out how I had damaged my older kids by not putting them on their stomachs each day when they were tiny. I learned that the back of babies' heads can flatten from spending too much time on their backs. This started happening more often after the edict to put babies to sleep on their backs to reduce the risk of SIDS. Even though my kids seemed to have come out all right—so far—was it possible that I was doing this baby thing wrong?

The more I thought about it, the more I realized that all three of my babies had spent tons of time on their bellies: across

Some moms are information junkies, consuming research the way some of us plow through bowls of Ben & Jerry's.

my knees as I talked to friends at the park, propped on my husband's forearm as he walked around the house, and down on the floor, too, though I'd never timed it. William was lifting and turning his head, like he was supposed to. I was already doing it right. I needed to trust myself, which brings us to my next happiness secret: Gather information, but trust your gut.

Some moms are information junkies, consuming research the way some of us plow through bowls of Ben & Jerry's. Others turn to fellow moms or are drawn to an expert's viewpoint. All are great ways to get in the know. Focusing too much on a single source of information can have pitfalls, though. Doing your own research can be exhausting. Your favorite expert's discipline technique might stop your first child's tantrums before the second kick but make your youngest child scream louder. (Isn't it funny that no matter how loudly they're screaming, they can always manage to scream louder?) The mothers at back-to-school night may have "foolproof" ways they help their children focus on homework after school, but only you can decide if their methods are right for your kids.

Considering opinions that come at you from every direction (especially downwind from where certain relatives live) can be overwhelming. Happy mothering goes hand in hand with the knowledge that we can't take everyone's advice and that, even if we make mistakes (which we will), our kids will most likely turn out healthy, happy, and wise. Or at least smart enough to stop eating paste by, say, third or fourth grade. Or fifth.

Take the quiz on page 42 to identify your info-gathering style, then come back here for ideas on gathering intel, staying firmly in charge, and still having the energy to say, "If I have to tell you to be quiet one more time, we're turning this car around!"

We can't know everything

When your mother was young (don't tell her she isn't!), so-called "expert" parenting advice was limited. Sure, she may have carried around a dog-eared copy of a Dr. Spock book. But studies weren't coming down the pipeline every day, and news didn't travel in real time. Nowadays, we're supposed to keep up on an endless number of topics, from the benefits of teaching toddlers Mandarin to the latest recall on canned Mandarin orange segments—the list goes on and on.

Talk about pressure! If endless information is available, and it is, it can feel like there's no excuse for not making the "best"

"When my first son was a baby, the woman at the shoe store tried to convince us that children 'need' shoes to develop strong ankles. I didn't put shoes on him until he was fully walking. I let his ankles develop on their own. That woman must have forgotten that, for thousands of years, people were perfectly healthy and strong without brand-name shoes!" -Abigail

Q/A

What's your info style?

When in doubt, do you consult the grapevine or Google for answers to your parenting questions?

1 *During your frustrating parenting moments, what do you do?*
   a. Head to the parenting section at the bookstore or pick up a parenting magazine.
   b. Search the website of your favorite expert, Dr. Smith, to find out her take on the topic.
   c. Ask the moms at playgroup what they think.

2 *At the playground, moms are talking about cloth vs. disposable diapers. You:*
   a. Bring up the data from an environmental study you read. (Then wonder why people ask you if Miranda Hobbes was your favorite *Sex and the City* character.)
   b. Quote Dr. Smith, who says it's perfectly fine to use disposable diapers.
   c. Say you use cloth but admit that your sister thinks it's a waste of time.

3 *The last few nights, your eight-year-old has been afraid to go to sleep. You:*
   a. Check a couple of books on bedtime issues and create an action plan for tackling the problem.
   b. Call the Dr. Smith show and ask for advice, under an assumed name, of course.
   c. Post it on Facebook and sort through feedback from a dozen friends, your aunt, and that guy you sat behind in physics. (Does he still wear acid-washed jeans?)

4 *Which of the following statements is most likely to come out of your mouth?*
   a. "I read a book last week that said that TV impairs infants' brain function."

b. "Dr. Smith says toddlers can be toilet trained by age three, so I'm not worried that Rory will be out of diapers by preschool."

c. "What do you do with your kids?"

5 *Your Yahoo! News says that sunscreen may cause cancer. You:*

a. Read what the American Academy of Pediatrics says on the issue and skim the section on sun safety on the other vetted sites you have bookmarked.

b. Check out Dr. Smith's website.

c. See what your favorite mom bloggers are saying about it.

Quiz key

Mostly A's: Data Diva Up on the latest stats and studies, you believe you can never have too much information.

Mostly B's: Guru Groupie You've found a trusted expert or two to whom you go for advice.

Mostly C's: Mother Superior When it comes to in-the-trenches parenting advice, you figure nobody's a better expert than another mom.

Were you an A, B, or C—or a mix of the three? Babies don't come preprogrammed, so it's normal to want to seek out advice when you're a parent. And no matter how you like to do your digging, it's fantastic that you've found effective ways to gather information. Parenting books, trustworthy experts, and other parents can all be great sources. Read on for more tips on how to research while trusting your gut and avoiding info overload.

"If you are comfortable taking your baby out, then do it. If you're worried about germs, bring a bottle of hand sanitizer and make anyone who wants to touch the baby clean up first. Unless you have a secret tunnel from the hospital to your house, your baby has already been 'out.' Don't let others intimidate you, do what you're comfortable with!" -3BoysMom

choice in every situation. Whatever that means. Knowledge is power, but the ability to roll with the punches and listen to your gut is the path to successful—and happy—motherhood. Here are a few tips for dealing with information overload:

Seek out information on a need-to-know basis. Product recalls and updated child-safety-seat information fall under "need to know." But a study conducted with 12 people that suggests a link between eating peas while pregnant and your child's crazy-long toes doesn't. If you can't do anything about the data or aren't sure the info matters, you probably don't need it.

Choose sources carefully. The Internet has made everyone and her sister a publisher, but that doesn't mean everything out there is worth reading (this book excluded, of course). Pare down your perusing, both online and in print, to a small number of trusted sources. Believe me, if something is really important, you'll hear about it one way or another.

Think it through. Even studies and stats from reliable sources don't always tell the whole story. And recommendations can frequently and rapidly change and evolve. If you read something that conflicts with your parenting philosophy, ask yourself: Is what I'm doing working? Is my child healthy and happy? Is there a compelling reason to switch things up?

Somebody will always disagree—and that's fine

Have you ever felt pressured to hide your child's battery-powered toys or move the cereals with the neon marshmallow nuggets to the back of the cupboard when pals are over? Do you practice "public discipline"—that is, give your five-year-old more time-outs in public than you do at home, so you don't seem like a pushover? Or the opposite, let her get away with more because she'll throw a crying fit if you give her a time-out? It's normal to want other parents to view you as a good mom. Problem is, everyone's definition of "good parenting" is different, so you can't be certain to please anyone but yourself.

When my kids were younger, I read a study that said kissing your children on the lips could promote tooth decay. Bacteria, it explained, travel from the mother's mouth to the child's, placing him or her at risk for cavities. An onslaught of mommy blog posts followed suggesting that we shouldn't be smooching our sweeties. No sloppy baby kisses? They're one of the best reasons for having kids. I still smooch. That doesn't mean that I was right and the nonkissing moms were wrong or vice versa.

We all have different tolerance levels for different kinds of risks. And our own experiences and priorities will always shape our decisions as parents. Nobody has all the answers. The key thing to remember is that it doesn't matter.

You are the #1 expert on your child

What do your mother, your best friend, your pediatrician, your boss, and (unless it's you) the parenting-book author on the *Today* show (please, oh, please let it be me) have in common? None of them knows your child better than you do. Their insights can be helpful, but no one else—except for Dad—gets the nuances of your child's needs the way you do. A child's

You see your child at his best, wrapping his arms around your neck for a super-duper-crazy-crusher hug.

parents are the best people to make the final call about what's right for him. After all, you're the ones who have seen him at his worst, kicking and screaming on the bathroom floor at Target, and at his best, wrapping his arms around your neck for a super-duper-crazy-crusher hug. You're putting in the time, and every day you're learning more and more about what makes your child tick. So trust yourself.

Some things are easier than others
You may find that you feel more confident in some areas, like discipline (counting to five may actually work with your kids),

"My pediatrician recommended that we try the 'cry it out' method for our son, but it backfired. He didn't fall asleep on his own, and his naps got shorter and more difficult. Eventually, we got our little one to sleep through our own trial and error. I wish doctors would realize that one method isn't right for every child!"
-BeccaV

and less in others, like family meals (your child takes being a picky eater to a whole new level).

Some parents feel confident until running into a rough stage, say puberty. All moms sometimes have to feel their way through lots of difficult decisions, like figuring out what to do with sibling rivalry gone wild or selecting the appropriate consequence for coming home after curfew. If there's a person who shakes your confidence in your own judgment, check out my favorite brush-offs, right, and then follow the steps below to help you master guilt-free decision-making for yourself.

Identify your obstacles

Is something getting in the way of your first choice for your child? Is this obstacle real or imagined? Some real ones: You and your husband disagree about what to do; the decision would affect the rest of your family; or it goes against most experts' advice. In contrast, here are some obstacles that don't matter in the long run: dissenting friends, disagreeing relatives, or the opinion of some random expert on the radio. If there's a real obstacle, you'll have to jump over it (or scoot around it, the way your kid scoots around that heap of Tinkertoys with his Big Wheel, instead of, heaven forbid, actually cleaning up the mess). Here's how to navigate the smackdown:

You vs. Dad. You win! Yay! Okay, just kidding—you didn't really think it was going to be that easy, did you? First, try to figure out if Dad's actually disagreeing by hearing him out. Give him that courtesy, and then explain your point of view. Try to resist becoming defensive, especially if you're divorced. You share the same goal: doing the best thing for your kids. There are a lot of reasons why couples disagree on parenting approaches. Sometimes those arguments are really about other issues. Check out chapter 10 for more on dealing with Dad.

Your gut instinct vs. science. You gotta have a few trusted sources for vital health and safety info, like how much Tylenol

Five ways to (nicely) blow off busybodies

Here are some strategies for responding to unsolicited advice without feeling like you have to change what you're doing:

1 **Soften your "no" with nostalgia**
Grandma: "My mother would have washed out my mouth with soap!" *You: "Isn't it funny how parenting approaches have changed over the years?"*

2 **Humor them**
Mother-in-law: "I read that kids who do their own dishes don't do as well in school!" *You: "Hmm, interesting. I'll think that over."*

3 **Reinforce your authority**
Neighbor: "You aren't going to let your son ride his bike to school, are you? It's so dangerous!" *You: "I've done a lot of safety research, and I'm comfortable with it."*

4 **Blame the expert**
Childcare provider: "I really think she should be potty training by now." *You: "I talked to my pediatrician, and she agreed it's better to wait until she's a little older."*

5 **Provide a diversion**
Cashier: "You know, if you buy them candy when they ask, they'll never stop bossing you around." *You: "Wasn't that box of macaroni supposed to be on sale?"*

to give your three-year-old, or what to do if your child does a triple flip off the monkey bars and lands on his head. (But, gosh, his form earned him a perfect ten.) But the science surrounding some things, like the best solid food for babies, isn't nearly as cut-and-dried. Remember, you and your family are not a statistic, and if those people in the white coats really knew it all, there would be a chocolate bar that cures mommy muffin-tops. Talk to your pediatrician when you have questions and bookmark a reliable website such as AAP.org (American Academy of Pediatrics) for after-hours nonurgent questions.

Sometimes happy motherhood means deciding to buck a convention and do things your way.

One family member's needs vs. another's. This is one of the toughest conflicts. Your family is a unit, and your decisions have to take everyone's needs into account, not only the squeakiest wheel. Let's say you found a fantastic private school for your oldest child. But paying for the tuition will mean you'll have to put off preschool for your youngest. That kind of choice is hard to make, so try to focus on the here and now: Make the decision based on what's best for you and your family at this moment. When weighing the options, put yourself in your child's shoes and think about her current needs, even if they're not what you anticipated initially.

What's important to you?

If after considering any real obstacles, you're still not sure what to do, take a closer look at your priorities. Yours may not be the same as someone else's. For instance, your best friend might feel it's really important to give her kids music lessons starting in kindergarten, while your sister-in-law thinks there's nothing more valuable than free play at that age. If you lined up a hundred sets of great parents in a row and asked them to list their top five must-dos, I bet they would all have different answers. Dig deep for your own.

Also ask yourself if the issue can wait. Maybe you were convinced that you'd be ready to go back to work full time when your son started first grade, but now you aren't feeling so great about it. Your afternoons together have come to mean a lot to you. What would happen if you simply did nothing for now? You can always revisit the issue in a week or a month.

Follow your own beat

Our moms outfitted us in orthopedic shoes. We put math-game apps on our smart phones so we can teach Junior precalculus while we're in the grocery-store checkout line. Every generation has its parenting trends. But sometimes, happy motherhood means deciding to buck a convention and do things your way. Who knows? You could start the next big thing.

It's not always easy to trust your inclinations! In my early years of motherhood, I sometimes found myself waffling on whether to shun red dye #5 or if my child was ready for sleepovers, based on what some study suggested or my friends thought. But in the end, all I could do was go with what my instincts were telling me.

Even though I've made a lot of boo-boos along the way—the kind no mommy kiss or Scooby Doo bandage can fix—my kids are turning out fine. And while I may have resorted to bribing them once or twice (the United Nations could stand to learn a thing or two about the peacekeeping powers of a handful of Skittles), they don't seem to be growing up into minimobsters. No, my boys didn't master the potty by age two, but they didn't go to kindergarten in diapers, either. To me, that's the epitome of being flush with success.

In a typical month, we moms make a million decisions big and small. Over the years, we'll do a lot of things right and also mess up some details along the way—it all evens out in the end. So have the confidence to experiment until you figure out what works for you and your kids. After all, you're the expert.

Ask three people you trust, plus your kids if they're talking, why they think you're a terrific mom. Write down their answers along with your own thoughts. Read them whenever you're feeling uncertain or less than rosy about motherhood.

4

keep it real

If you take your cues from paper-towel commercials, then moms are women with high-waisted pants who love to clean. Except celebs, of course. They have flawless skin and return to their jam-packed filming schedules faster than you can find the Wii remote under the sofa cushions. And, of course, let's not forget the mommy bloggers who are as fresh-faced as their children, frolicking on their organic farms.

Oh, I know you get that Hollywood is a land of make-believe, except with plastic surgeons and personal trainers, and that the bloggers' kids have goat poop on their shoes. But the more pictures you see of the handwoven straw fairy cottages and unchipped mani-pedis, the easier it becomes to delude yourself into thinking you might be missing out on something.

I've succumbed to the pull of searching for a mom-dentity, myself. At first, I tried to turn into an über–Earth Mother. I imagined my kids' lives as a free-floating utopia with a Dan Zanes soundtrack and a wealth of hands-on nature experiences. But what I got was paint smears on the table, mud on the carpet, and a bad case of burnout.

I was miserable. Not because I don't like singing or macaroni art, but because I was pushing myself to do those things even when I didn't feel like it. Truth is, I'd rather play checkers than wade in a creek spur-of-the-moment. I was trying to be somebody I'm not, and it backfired.

Reality programming

My fourth secret to happiness is to "keep it real." And doing so isn't always as easy as it should be. There's a balancing act to perform. On one side, keeping it real means not clinging to every last aspect of your prepregnancy self, even though there's plenty of pressure to do so. Certainly the media lay it on thick: Stars who get back to their before-baby weight within a month get plastered over the cover of every celeb mag on the newsstand—inevitably wearing a dress that looks more like a large belt and sky-high stilettos.

And doesn't everyone love (okay, secretly resent and fear, but *pretend* to love) that coworker who gives birth to triplets and still spends her vacation in South America building houses for the poor? Well, phooey to all that. It's silly to think that kids won't interrupt our lives to some degree (after all, they interrupt our phone calls!). Motherhood demands a lot of attention and resources, and no mom has the time to pursue everything she used to.

That being said, you're not keeping it real if you jettison all your favorite aspects of your pre-mom self. It's important to keep this stuff intact, like your sense of humor or your trademark habit of sending friends surprise "thinking of you" cards. Having kids doesn't suddenly change your DNA. It won't magically make you love leading little plastic people on a tour of the Lollipop Woods, but it also doesn't mean you're now too grown-up to play Ms. Pac-Man at the pizza parlor arcade and pile the parmesan on your slice of pepperoni. Rather than trying to live up to your own—or anyone else's—idea of what a "good mom" is, embrace the mom you are. She's even better!

How about you? How do you keep it real? The quiz on page 54 will help you find out if you're more real-you than reality-star.

The quiz on page 54 will help you find out if you're more real-you than reality-star.

{ **mom to mom** }

"Sometimes, I'm Supermom, perfectly pressed cape in place, homemade cookies for the class party, kids with hair bows that match their socks. Other days, I'm Slacker Mom, serving cold cereal for dinner, with dirty floors, unmade beds, and frizzy hair. I can't compare myself to some idealized version of what 'Mother' should look like. I am far from the perfect mom, but I am the perfect mom for my kids." -*Kelsey*

keep it real **53**

Q/A

Will the real mom please stand up?

Being a mom means going through some changes, but it doesn't have to mean becoming another person. Where do you stand?

1 *After your baby was born, what happened to your old routine?*
   a. It went out the window—along with breakfast.
   b. Things were crazy at first, but then you started to read the newspaper again and got back into running.
   c. You barely missed a beat—or a single hour of sleep.

2 *When your daughter wants to participate in an activity that doesn't interest you, what do you do?*
   a. Jump in with both feet. Sure, you've always hated basketball, but that doesn't mean you can't coach a team of ten-year-olds, right? Right?
   b. Drive her to soccer practice, but cheer from the sidelines.
   c. Nix the idea entirely. Field hockey sounds borrring.

3 *You're chatting with another mom at your son's birthday party, and she mentions staying up all night to bake and decorate her daughter's cake. You glance at the store-bought cake sporting your son's name and think . . .*
   a. "Next year, I should make the cake myself."
   b. "Good for her, but I'd rather fingerpaint than bake!"
   c. "Baking cakes? I don't *think* so."

4 *You and your two-year-old go to a toddler music class. You've never considered the hokey pokey to be what it's all about. You:*
   a. Suffer in silence as you put your scowling face in and put your scowling face out.
   b. Give the class one more chance, and if you're still not having any fun, skip it for a weekly ice cream date.
   c. Do the hocus-pocus and disappear, or, better yet, never appear there in the first place. A toddler music class is not your scene.

5 *How much has motherhood changed your look?*
   a. Totally, from your haircut (wash and wear!) to your shoes (bye-bye Manolos, hello Merrells!).
   b. You wear more basics, are thrilled that Target has gotten so hip, and wear yoga pants even if today's agenda doesn't have room for any ohms.
   c. Not at all. Your Nordstrom personal shopper is on speed dial, and you have your roots touched up every month.

6 *Your daughter loves her new classmate, but you think her mom's annoying. How do you handle it?*
   a. Make friends with the woman anyway—you want the kids to be close, and you're pretty sure you can get used to her laugh. Giggle! Snort!
   b. Invite the kid's family over for a barbecue. Who knows, it's possible that the mom's actually funny. If not, you'll stick with kid-only get-togethers afterward.
   c. Encourage your child to find other friends whose moms are more on your wavelength.

Quiz key

Mostly A's: Woman, Interrupted Your old identity is dying to bust out of the mom jeans you've zipped her into.

Mostly B's: Yours Truly You've shoved over some of your indie CDs to make room for *Yo Gabba Gabba!*, but you're still you.

Mostly C's: Status Quo–Conscious Holding on to parts of your pre-kid identity is important, but it's also good to embrace the positive changes that come with being a mom.

[**did you know**]

Hopefully the quiz helped you learn a little bit more about yourself—and about what your new motto should be. Like the old song says, "Hold on loosely, but don't let go." Let's take a closer look at the payoffs.

Boldly go where you've never gone before

Chances are, when you first found out you were pregnant, you spent lots of time imagining all the things you'd help your child discover and learn to love—swing sets and swim classes, Build-A-Bears and birthday cakes. But did you ever think about the stuff you'd discover too?

Star Trek didn't get it quite right: Rugrats, not Romulans, are the final frontier, urging us to explore strange new worlds—ones filled with brightly colored snacks and mysterious trading cards featuring anime creatures. Boldly go where so many moms have gone before and sample the things your child loves; you'll be better for it. Honest.

Trying unfamiliar things with your kid offers you a huge opportunity to discover new things that you like, whether it's miniature golf, Crazy 8, or those can't-eat-just-one veggie puffs that look like packing peanuts. And that can make you a

If the scenario ends without anyone bleeding, throwing up, or ruining any dry-clean-only clothing, it's worth giving it a try.

happier mom, since the list of things that you know you can fall back on when you need a boost will expand. For example, say you consider "roughing it" to be a motel that doesn't serve free breakfast. But your budding seven-year-old naturalist wants to spend a night, ugh, in a tent. While it might be tempting to send Dad out to the woods with the bug spray—after all, your sense of adventure has never really extended beyond the length of your hair-dryer cord—consider giving it the old college try: Your kids will appreciate the effort, you'll have more opportunities to bond, and you'll model a spirit of adventure and openness.

Make it your own

Need a little more help psyching yourself up? Here are some tips for learning to enjoy new things with your kids. It might be the beginnings of a great new mother-child hobby you'll do together for years. Or it might make for a funny story later. Either way you win.

Ask yourself what's the worst that could happen. Say you said "yes" to playing in the rain or entering a family spelling bee. Imagine the scenario in your head. If it ends without anyone bleeding, throwing up, or ruining any dry-clean-only clothing, it's at least worth giving it a try. Anyway, if you don't enjoy yourself, no one says you'll have to do these things every day.

Don't put too much of your money where your mouth is. Your daughter is begging you to take her for a bike ride; you aren't sure you even remember how to balance. Before plunking down hundreds of dollars for a new bike, ask a neighbor if you can take hers for a spin, or rent one for a few hours.

Look for the upside. Sure, going to the beach means you'll need to vacuum sand out of the car afterward. But you'll get to sit in the sun for an hour, and your kids will wear themselves out so thoroughly they'll take a record-length nap when you get home. When you focus on the positives, you might decide that a little grit is a worthwhile trade-off.

Try, try, and try again. I give myself three chances to like something before I give it up forever. Think of it this way: During that first Mommy and Me class, everybody's feeling awkward. During the second, you're still going through a learning curve. By the third, you should know some of the songs, remember a few moms' names, and know whether you want to come back—or not.

"I was never athletic and never thought I'd be a 'soccer mom.' Now I love going to my daughter's games. I'm sad when soccer season ends."
-Angela

You + momhood = awesome

Maybe your boobs are making a run for your belly button and your Mini Cooper has been replaced by a minivan. But think of the good stuff that motherhood has taught you:

1 **Confidence.** Even the most conflict-shy mom will quickly turn into a roaring mama bear when her baby cub needs her. Grrr!

2 **Compassion.** Once upon a time, you would have glared at the mom with the screaming child on a packed 747. Never again, now that you know how that feels.

3 **Focus.** Hey, you're busy raising productive members of society here. Who has time for things that don't matter, like drama in the parent section of the bleachers?

4 **Organization.** Ditch fears that you'll become a frazzled, forgetful mom. Motherhood actually makes us smarter and more efficient. Bonus!

5 **Patience.** This one's a toughie, but with kids, you get lots of chances to practice slowing down and learning to react calmly when things take a less-than-ideal turn.

Choose what you like

All right, so you're trying new stuff to see what you like—good for you! Who knows, it may inspire your picky middle schooler to try Brussels spr . . . oh, who are we kidding? But just because you've decided to see what else is out there for you, that doesn't mean you've got to stick with it. Yes, you became a mom, but you're still you, y'know? The choice is completely yours. Try new activities and interests, but stick with them only if you enjoy them and they don't crowd out your long-standing favorites. (See chapter 9, "Look out for #1," for tips on fitting those interests into your life.)

Not everything you try will make the cut. Perhaps you expected to relax at mom-and-baby yoga, but the cacophony of crying infants made you crave a choir's tunes instead. In that case, you might be better off doing a few Downward Dogs at home. Or maybe you've decided you don't like yoga. Who cares if Gwyneth—or that Demi Moore lookalike in your book club—says it gave her back her abs, or that all the other moms on your street swear by it?

Also, there are some experiences—like the "joy" of sucking on those so-sour-they-hurt candies or racking up points playing Cash Cow on Webkinz—that kids can appreciate on their own. And family, friends, other kids, and school can be great ways to expose your kids to something you don't enjoy. Having your math-whiz neighbor help your son with his algebra homework, in return for you helping her son with his English essay, saves you both wear and tear.

Your child's favorite mom

These tactics are all great tricks, and they'll help you pull off a bigger one: letting motherhood change you for the better and the happier, not turn you into a completely new person. So don't be afraid to be who you really, truly are—even if you don't multitask as well as Claire Huxtable, can't fly a kite to save your life, or don't particularly love Dr. Seuss.

(easy jump start)

At dinner, have everyone write down five things they'd like to do as a family, like trying a new restaurant or going water skiing. This week, use those ideas to compile a family wish list, and check off one new activity.

5

find your tribe

What's on your list of mommy must-haves? A first-aid kit? Check. The cell number of a babysitter with CPR training and no current boyfriend? Check. A car that has every airbag known to automotive science but doesn't look too dorky? Check.

But how about a support group—a collection of friends (and maybe family members, too) who pull for you in tough times and stir the margarita mix when you want to have fun? A tribe like that ought to rank among your essentials as well. Sure, a first-aid kit is important, but so is a pal to wield the tweezers when you've got a tick between your shoulder blades. (Don't ask me how I know this.)

It's not easy to find the energy to invest in friends when you barely have time to brush your teeth.

My fifth secret: Find your tribe. All moms need some peeps to lean on. It's vital to your happiness—see "margarita mix," above—which in turn makes you a better mom. It can even make you healthier: One of the biggest risk factors for postpartum depression, and depression in general, is isolation. The bottom line is that you don't have to go it alone.

But it's not easy to find the energy to invest in friends when you barely have time to brush your teeth. With your packed schedule, who could blame you if your social circle has dwindled to a few moms with kids the same age as yours? Or maybe you're not sure what's the best way to meet new people. In today's rush-rush culture, making friends isn't as easy as asking a neighbor for an egg, but it can be done. In this chapter, we'll talk about how to find and keep amazing pals.

Types of friends every mom needs

A strong network of friends is about more than the number of contacts in your smart phone. No matter if you like to be in the middle of a crowd or would rather nurture a few close ties, you need more than one kind of buddy. Here's a list of the friends you've gotta have.

The there-in-a-heartbeat pal She's the one who's willing to suffer through a dozen dressing-room breakdowns before you find a flattering blouse—and then bring you one of hers at work when you discover that said blouse has a glob of rice-cereal-turned-cement on the front. Make it a point to express appreciation for a go-to friend and to reciprocate in your own way, so that your buddy doesn't start feeling like the relationship is a one-way street. (If you've been guilty of doing this, see "Lost and Found" on page 70, where I'll help you perform CPR on a friendship that's in critical condition.)

The right-where-you-are buddy This friend is happy to hash out the how-old-should-kids-be-before-they-get-a-cell-phone issue (for the 15th time) or agree enthusiastically while you marvel over your preschooler's cute lisp (for the 50th time). She is another mom who's going through the same phases as you are. These friendships can be a challenge to hang on to if one mom's circumstances change. If you used to meet at the playground at 10 AM but your friend gets a full-time job, try to hook up in the evening or on weekends instead, so that neither of you loses that valuable connection.

The BTDT buddy One trap newer moms tend to fall into is hanging out only with other newbies. But "been there, done that" vets of the wake-up-it's-time-for-school battle are wonderful sources of practical advice and emotional support. They know what's worth worrying about (your daughter's

Q/A

Who ya gonna call?

Do you have all the friends a mom needs? Ask yourself:

1 *If something major happened—marital trouble, a sticky issue at work—whom could you confide in?*

2 *Daycare closed down due to a power outage, and you have a can't-miss meeting. Is there someone you can ask to watch your kids . . . even if she knows that will mean a morning of dancing to the* Barney Perfectly Platinum 30 Dino-Mite Songs *CD?*

3 *Is there someone on your speed dial whom you can call for minor problems—like what does "festive attire" mean?*

4 *You're stir crazy and have to get out of the house. Who will race you to the nearest Starbucks?*

5 *When your child takes her first steps, who (after Dad) is next on your list for a phone call?*

6 *If you need an opinion about whether it's time to hit the gym more often, who'll make you do a 360 and then give you her honest, uh, hindsight?*

Okay, assuming you had an answer for every scenario (and if you did, you're doing better than a lot of us), go back and re-read the questions. This time, assume that the first person you named is not available. How'd you do? Is it maybe time to expand your circle?

sudden secretive texting) and what isn't (the fact that the Tooth Fairy forgot to stop by your six-year-old's pillow last night). That said, even the most patient Dear Abby–type friend isn't all about her brilliant advice; you can—and should!—call her to talk about shared non-kid interests, like politics.

The tells-it-like-it-is ally We all need at least one friend who tells it to you straight—your sister, a friend who's known you forever, or a newer pal who's great at giving you the lowdown. This is the gal who isn't afraid to tell you not to send a "How are you doing?" Facebook message to that old boyfriend who dumped you, and to stop worrying about whether your child's clothes match. You may not always want to hear your friend's opinion, but there's a good chance she's right.

Make sure you tell her how much you value her honesty, and even if you don't do what she suggests, let her know you appreciate her advice. That doesn't mean you have to endure endless disapproval, though. Friendships like these only work

A true friend will tell you not to send a Facebook message to that old boyfriend who dumped you.

when the advice-giver mixes praise with her criticism—and she should be willing to take what she dishes out (or at least be honest enough about herself to admit she can't).

The child-free friend Who else can dish about the latest celeb break-up now that your bathroom reading is *Parenting* instead of *People*? This pal also doesn't have to get a babysitter and is probably up for a night out after you tuck in your cherubs. Remember, though, a friend who's not used to kids might get annoyed when you pause in the middle of a juicy bit of gossip to tell your kids to stop putting crayons in the DVR. And stuff you've become blasé about, like poop and snot rockets, likely aren't her idea of good dinner-table conversation.

Still, motherhood is a huge part of who you are, and she can't expect you to act like it isn't. So tell that story about your toddler accidentally flipping off your mother-in-law, but make it short and sweet, and then ask your pal about her love life.

Making friends 101

So now you know the kinds of friends you need, but making them might be easier said than done. How do you connect with another mom while you're clapping along with "The Wheels on the Bus" during Mini Mozart class? If your kids play in the middle-school band together, how do you know if you've got anything in common in the brief breaks between "Beethoven's Fifth" and, well, whatever that screechy tune they're playing is supposed to be?

It can be intimidating, but you can do it. You're still that same person who had friends in elementary school. (And if you didn't have many friends back then, don't worry: These days, your mom doesn't make you carry a Holly Hobbie lunch box.)

**How do you connect with another mom while you're
clapping along with "The Wheels on the Bus"?**

Speaking of school, your parent-teacher organization can be a great way to meet the moms of your kids' friends. If you work outside the home, of course, it can be harder to exploit this angle, since you can't be as active during the day in the classroom. That's where bleachers and auditorium seats come in. During a baseball game or school talent show, ask your neighbor, "So, which one is yours?" and take it from there.

If your kids are pre-K, one of the best ways to find mom friends is to join a parent group with other moms of kids the same age as your own little one. Check with local hospitals, look for flyers at toy stores or baby boutiques, or scan online forums to find moms getting together in your area.

Six ways even shy moms can make connections

1 Be helpful. As another mom's talking, keep your mental Rolodex flipping. Is she complaining she can't find a good yoga studio? Nab her number and invite her to try yours with you—she may be your "ohm" girl before you know it.

2 Try technology. Put an e-mail list together to keep the conversation going after Mommy and Me.

3 Use your kids as an excuse. "Look how nicely Sam and Maya get along! We should get them together again."

4 Ask for help hooking up. You know that friend or sister who seems to know everyone? Ask her to introduce you to people she thinks you'd like.

5 Be there. Mention that you're always at step class at 11 AM on Tuesdays, then make sure you show up.

6 Share your digits. Carry a pen and Post-it notes in your purse, send an e-mail from your smart phone right away to exchange e-mail addresses, or even make your own "calling cards." Whichever way you prefer, be ready to swap contact info with soon-to-be pals!

Not every acquaintance is destined to be your BFF. Your potential buddy may be too busy to get back to you. If the ball lands with a thud in the other mom's court, don't take it personally—dust yourself off and try again.

You can try starting a club, whether your hobby is quilting, playing volleyball, or doing improv, or join an existing one at a craft store, gym, or community theater. My experience has taught me that book clubs, an obvious choice, have a way of turning into happy-hour chatfests, but you might make some great friends even if you do spend more time talking about Charles and Camilla than Charles Dickens.

Online friends can be a boon for moms because they fit in your schedule. You can be on the computer late at night, between feedings, or while the kids are at school. One note of caution: The Internet offers great ways to connect and keep in touch with other moms, but be careful about replacing real-life friends with online relationships. If your live-to-online friend balance gets out of whack, ask yourself what you value most about cybercompanionship and see if you can find that in your own backyard. Try scaling back your time online and using some of that time to visit a friend or make a phone call.

Don't clique

We'd all like to think we left cliques and petty jealousies behind in high school, but it's easy to feel like you're in no-moms-land when you're trying to crack the social code in the neighborhood or at your child's school. Suddenly, all those insecurities you thought you left behind rise up to the surface. (It's your hair, right? Or maybe your shoes?)

The good news is, you're a grown-up now. If you're dying to infiltrate that gaggle of moms whose kids have known each other practically since birth, what have you got to lose? Put aside those fears, walk up, say "hello," and introduce yourself. Trust me, they're not going to put a "kick me" sign on your back. And if you find that they aren't receptive, create your own clan, one buddy at a time. Before you know it, you'll have your own group of girlfriends to lean on. And when you do, remember how lonely it can feel to be on the fringes and reach out to other moms who look as uncertain as you once felt.

Putting the "end" in "friend"

Between searching for lost Legos and keeping sibling tickling matches from dissolving into crying-and-pants-peeing sessions, you've got enough drama. Yes, friendship takes effort, but if keeping a certain friend happy (or around!) feels like a full-time job, there's a good chance it's not working.

Some signs it may be time to slacken or even cut ties: You struggle to stay in touch, she cancels last-minute for less-than-urgent reasons, she does most of the talking, or your get-togethers leave you feeling depleted instead of energized. If you feel like a friend takes more from the relationship than she's willing to give, or if you feel bad about yourself after spending time together, it may be worth reconsidering the friendship.

Shedding friends never is easy, but—like cleaning out the veggie bin and braving a three-way mirror in a tankini—it's sometimes necessary. If you get a sinking feeling when a pal's number flashes on your caller ID, you may find that you have to do some breaking up. Cool-offs may not be permanent;

Shedding friends never is easy, but—like cleaning out the veggie bin—it's occasionally necessary.

there's a chance you'll find one another later. But some friendships aren't built to go the distance, and that's okay, too.

Either way, leave your options open and make the separation gentle. Ease out of it by spending less time with your friend, letting her know that your schedule is jam packed, and suggesting that it might make more sense for you to get back to her if your schedule opens up. Be kind—but not available.

How to get on anyone's A list

The best way to make a good friend is to be one. Even if your time and patience are limited, you can show your buddies you

Lost and found

It happens to the best of buddies: Life gets crazy, you miss a phone call or six, and now you feel too sheepish to reach out again. But really good friends stay connected down deep, even when life gets between them. It doesn't matter whose "fault" the cooling-off was—if the friendship is important to you, try sending an e-mail or picking up the phone.

If it's reached the point where an out-of-the-blue call seems too awkward, wait for her birthday and send a card with a thoughtful gift. You'll never regret trying to reconnect with a person who's important to you. Some more ideas: Mail an old photo of the two of you that you "happened" to come across, surprise her with a little gift of something she likes (like that strawberry-rhubarb jam you know she loves), or even put your child on the phone to say a quick "hi" as an icebreaker. Who could say "no" to that?

care by being thoughtful. Text your neighbor from the grocery store to see if she needs milk, offer to drive another parent's kids home after choir practice, or send your high school best friend a magazine article that made you think of her. Maybe you could make the surprise even more special by sending it via snail mail—charming these days. And if a friend's Facebook status indicates she's having a hard time, send her a private message or give her a call. When your friend is thinking about adopting a new hobby or tackling a career goal, be encouraging—one of the best gifts we can give a friend is faith in her goals, so give her a thumbs up and offer to watch her kids after school on days she may have to work late.

Hands-on support is almost always welcome, and don't wait to be asked: When you're hanging out at her house, offer to help fold the laundry or stack the dishwasher while you talk. You can also take your friend's kids off her hands—an hour of child-free grocery shopping can feel like heaven. Better yet, take her kids for a couple of hours in the evening and return them bathed, in their PJs, and ready for bed.

Friends forever

Don't underestimate how much a small gesture can help a friend who's having a rough time of it or a crummy evening. And even when you're losing it a little yourself, it's amazing sometimes how manageable it is to help somebody else. Who knows, reaching out may give you a little boost of feel-good energy that will help you get your own stuff back together too.

A posse is a must-have for every mom. It's true: Diaper blowouts during church are more hilarious when you relate them to a friend after the fact, and your tween's Jekyll-and-Hyde demeanor feels less frustrating when your friend's kid is acting exactly the same and you can swap stories. With some creativity and effort, you can gather your own tribe of supporters to lean on through ups and downs—and in turn be that friend that every other mother needs too.

Did another mom do something nice for you lately, like finding a lollipop in her purse to rescue you from a toddler meltdown? Send a brief note of thanks (e-mail is fine). You'll feel good—and make her day.

6

go with the flow

We've all been there. Your plan seemed perfectly reasonable: Drop your son off at karate, swing by the grocery store, pick up the dry cleaning, retrieve your son. You didn't know your son would forget his belt, the cleaner wouldn't be able find your shirt, and the car would start making a noise you could only describe as a bison in heat (though you'll later learn it's actually the sound of $487 about to leave your emergency account).

Is there any way to save the evening? Sure—if you go with the flow, the sixth secret to being a happier mom. Having kids means our lives are always a little bit out of control. It's tempting to try to circumvent chaos by clamping down even harder. But as moms, the one thing we can plan for is that things won't always go according to plan. We have a choice: stick to the itinerary and be in a constant state of panties-in-a-twist, or refuse to let that sort of metaphoric underwear malfunction happen.

Being flexible is more than just resisting the temptation to jam-pack your daily schedule—it's a state of mind. With children, change is unavoidable and unexpected. For example: Your daughter can't extricate herself from her leotard fast enough and pees on her tights an hour before the big recital. Do you freak out? Borrow tights from a friend? Or call Dad to pick up a pair at the nearest drugstore?

Sometimes when a crisis strikes, all we can do is take a deep breath, remind ourselves that everything will be okay in the end, and figure out a strategy. It doesn't have to be a perfect solution (a brand-new dance outfit!), but simply the next-best thing (dry tights that look reasonably close to the other kids'). Losing it over wet tights wastes time you could use to load batteries into the camera and give your little ballerina a good-luck hug, and a freak-out is likely to put you—and everyone around you—into a stressed-out, anxious mood.

Of course, calmly steering into motherhood's ever-changing current (instead of gripping the raft in terror and frantically trying to paddle away) is a lot easier when you set your life up to allow for last-minute changes and crises. Whether you've got your days planned down to each granola-bar dispersal or can barely remember which day it is, here are some tips to help you find the right amount of flexibility, so every day's a little smoother, saner—and of course, happier!

Plan weeks, not days

There are only 24 hours in a day, and it's easy for the hunt for a lost utility bill to sap the time and energy you need for other things you'd hoped to accomplish. Just as pediatricians advise us to judge a picky child's diet by what he eats over the course of a week rather than a single 24-hour period, it helps to apply a bigger-picture attitude to our must-do (and want-to-do) plans and activities.

It's okay to loosely plan to hit the wholesale club on Monday, aquarium on Tuesday, school book fair on Wednesday, and so on, but be prepared to switch things up at a few minutes' notice. If it's 70 degrees and sunny today, you can watch the high school football game instead of going to the store without feeling like a procrastinator. And when your preschooler takes a rare afternoon nap, it won't seem like such a big deal to visit the clownfish a little later in the week. To find out how you feel about going with the flow, take the quiz on page 76.

To find out how you feel about going with the flow, take the quiz on page 76.

{ **mom to mom** }

"I worried a lot with my first child especially, but once I had another, I started saying, 'Oh, little Timmy fell on the sidewalk and skinned his knees—no biggie!' I'll always worry about the important stuff, but slowly, I've learned to let the everyday stuff slide. It's all new, and we're learning as mothers!"
-*MyBoysMom*

go with the flow **75**

Q/A

What's your flex factor?

The nanny cancels at 8 AM. Your teen tumbles off her bike. Yes, parenthood is rife with surprises. Do you roll with the punches or run for cover?

1 *While you're cooking dinner, your two-year-old tries to flush his shoe down the toilet. By the time you've saved his sneaker from a swirly, the meal is burned. What to do?*
   a. Improvise. Breakfast for dinner, anyone?
   b. Say a four-letter word (which your kids will then chant in front of Grandma on her next visit). So much for planning a week of menus on Sunday.
   c. Dinner? Is it 6 PM already?

2 *You're grocery shopping when your child throws a screaming, head-banging, leg-kicking fit. You:*
   a. Make a beeline for the cashier, even though you're only halfway through your shopping list. You wonder how tonight's lasagna will taste with no cheese in it.
   b. Grit your teeth and plod along, while shoppers all around give you the evil eye.
   c. Leave your half-full cart, pick up your kid, and head for the door.

3 *You were planning a casual dinner out with friends tonight, but your husband called to say he has to work late. You:*
   a. Invite your friends (and their children) to your house for an impromptu potluck. At least you'll finally be able to tell your mother-in-law that you used the fondue set she gave you for Christmas. (The leopard-print Snuggie is another matter.)
   b. Pitch a fit and start calling sitters.
   c. Resign yourself to missing (another) get-together.

4 *You wanted to take your kids to the library and museum today, but wake up to nasty weather. What do you do?*
   a. Cook up some salt clay instead.

b. Pull out the umbrellas and the raincoats. Gale force winds be damned.

c. You never make plans ahead of time.

5 *Even though you usually don't like to use TV as a babysitter, a last-minute work project has you scrambling for something to keep the kids occupied. You:*

a. Let them enjoy a *Dora the Explorer* marathon this time, so you don't end up exploring the unemployment office.

b. Stick to your guns, even though it means you'll have to stay up late and miss out on sleep (that's what caffeine and concealer are for).

c. Turn the TV on, and then get so involved in the project that you forget to ever turn it off. Or make dinner.

Quiz key

Mostly A's: You strike a balance between structured and soft. Relaxing bedtime every now and then or reworking your day when your toddler wakes up on the wrong side of the crib doesn't phase you.

Mostly B's: You'd never dream of giving in to a whim . . . or a whine . . . or a weather emergency. But letting the kids go to bed 15 minutes late every now and then won't turn them feral, and it might make your life a little easier.

Mostly C's: You'd say rules are made to be broken—if you had any rules to begin with. Flexibility is great, but if you're the human equivalent of a Silly Bandz, you might benefit from a bit more structure.

A stressful morning with
the kids is worse
than a bad day at work
for 55 percent of moms.
-Parenting.com

What did you learn from your quiz results? As a mom, life is full of surprises, and you never know when a piano teacher will arrive early or a client will forget a meeting. If you have a job with a rigid schedule, or if you don't have anyone to call for backup, time can feel even further out of your control. Here are some tips to help any mom stay calmer in the day-to-day rush.

Be vague

It's funny how kids always forget where they left their shoes, but they're like elephants when it comes to recalling that you promised them a treat. That is, they don't forget. Ever. So if there's any doubt at all about whether you'll be able to follow through on a promise, don't make it! Instead of saying, "We'll go to Dairy Queen after dinner," you could say, "We'll have ice cream sometime tonight." Then if the kids are too tired, hot, or cranky (or if you're too tired, hot, and cranky) to make a trip out, you can pull out a box of ice cream bars, hand them out to the kids, and let them drip all over the backyard while you kick your feet up and enjoy one, too.

While we're talking about making promises to people, don't forget friends, family, and coworkers. That yard sale you said you'd help your buddy with sounded so far away six weeks ago, but now it's this weekend and you're staring down two days of sitting in the hot sun haggling over her late great-uncle's deer antlers. I'm not saying never make a promise to help. But make sure the promise you make is something you can commit to. If an event is a long way off, consider all the possible conflicts that could make it difficult to keep your word.

Slim down your schedule

If you've got carpool at 3:15 PM, art lessons at 3:30 PM, soccer practice at 5 PM, and youth group at 7 PM, how could you possibly fit in a last-minute stop at the post office, or swing by the library to return an overdue book? With a schedule like that, even a trip through the drive-through to appease a thirsty kid can feel like a major detour.

Go from panic to peace

So your son forgot his science project at home—and didn't remember until you pulled into the school parking lot. How do you deal without falling apart?

1   **Take ten.** Seconds to calm down, that is. Turn off the car, turn on the radio, close your eyes, or step outside—whatever you need to move from rage to reason.

2   **Gather intel.** How important is it that this project be in today? What time does it need to be at the school by? Who could possibly help?

3   **Anticipate fallout.** If you drive home, you'll be late for work. If the project is late, your son's grade takes a hit. Both are rotten, but are they tragedies or annoyances?

4   **Consider alternatives.** Can your husband swing by home at lunchtime? Could your son take the lower grade? His homework is his responsibility, after all.

5   **Take action.** Once you have a plan, try to let it go. No point in fighting with your son (what's done is done) or being upset at work once you finally get there.

For years, parents have been sold the idea that we owe our kids a "leg up" by enrolling them in every enrichment activity possible, including foreign language classes, music lessons, tutoring, sports, ballet, or all of the above. Somewhere deep down, we probably all knew the go-go-go was kind of nuts, but it felt irresponsible to opt out. But these days, even trusted experts are telling parents to lay off. Kids need free time to play, think, and chill (so they don't get stressed out). Boredom teaches them to be creative. After all, who do you think first figured out that an empty milk carton makes a great sailboat? A bored kid, I bet!

Some kids and parents like to be busier than others, but bottom line: You don't owe your kids unlimited activities (that's Club Med, not Club Mom). In fact, you'll do them a service if you set some limits. In our house, the older children are allowed to be in one extracurricular at a time, and the younger children often don't do any formal classes at all, especially during the summer, when "low-effort living" is our family motto. We've found that we like checking out the local children's museum,

It may sound contradictory, but done right, a schedule actually gives life more flexibility.

going on nature hikes, talking, reading, and, yes, enjoying some educational television. Hey, today, I was watching Animal Planet and learned more about an eel's reproductive process than I ever thought possible.

Plan for flexibility

It may sound contradictory, but done right, a schedule actually makes life less, not more, rigid. A good calendar, organized systems for staying on top of everything, a list of priorities, and an understanding of your family's must-dos (and "eh, whatevers") are essential to cultivating flexibility. We'll talk more about planning—and how much easier it can make your life feel—in chapter 8. With these basics in place, going with the flow can become your natural state of mind.

And if you pencil in a block of time for "nothing"—it doesn't matter if it's on Wednesday morning or Saturday afternoon—you'll have wiggle room to handle the unexpected overflow stuff that came up during the week. Worst-case scenario, you'll use your free time removing gum from your daughter's hair. Best-case scenario? You can spend a few hours playing Old Maid, sipping lemonade in the backyard, or snuggling on the sofa with your child while you each read a book.

Cure for life's hiccups

If making these changes feels scary to you at first, then congratulations: You're doing it right. Giving up the illusion of control isn't always easy. Sometimes I feel like if I let one thing go, everything else will come tumbling down like a sticky house of cards. That's why I've found that it's easier to cope if I plan ahead a little. Putting off the grocery store for a day, for instance, won't work if you're down to a jar of mayonnaise and some moldy cheese. It pays to keep some staples handy—and I'm not only talking about groceries (though you could make do with the mayo and a can of tuna).

Let's be real here: Not everyone is naturally a "go with the flow" kind of person. If you are, it's more efficient to let life's little hiccups (a missed bus, burned biscuits) work themselves out. But if you aren't, you'll have to try a little harder at both setting up your life to accommodate those surprises and cultivating a life-won't-grind-to-a-halt-if-I-don't-buy-the-kids'-back-to-school-supplies-today mindset. Little things that help you stay prepared, like a list of babysitters, an extra change of clothes in the car, or a rainy-day board game, provide the freedom to fly by the seat of your pants when life hands you an unexpected storm. And anticipating that storm and staying calm as you weather it will allow you to react with something resembling poise—instead of panic—when it hits.

Think like Coco Chanel when making a to-do list: Write everything on it, then take one thing off.

7

make your bed

Before I had kids, I was never what you'd call neat. I wasn't even what Oscar the Grouch would call neat. Growing up, my closet looked like a crime scene. But disorder never seemed like that big a deal: All it took was a few hours to put everything where it was supposed to be, and I had the time to spare.

Then I had a baby. Suddenly my "free time" dissolved, as this little person came on the scene to undo all my tidying efforts—while making more than his own fair share of messes. I struggled along through kid number two, barely keeping my head above the tide of clutter (and my feet off the Play-Doh on the carpet) and always wondering why my home seemed like a wreck no matter how hard I tried to get it under control.

Bringing home my third baby was like being walloped over the head with the "get a clue" stick. I finally realized that keeping the house clean wasn't something I could schedule into neat little blocks of time after the kids were asleep (like sex!) or put off until the weekend (like sex!) or keep putting off forever (like, well, you know). Keeping the house under control had to become a way of life. The payoff: a home that lifts my spirits instead of filling me with dread that the doorbell would ring and someone—even the UPS person—would see the mayhem.

Don't get me wrong. My house is far from perfect, but it no longer qualifies as a Superfund site, either. Backpacks and toys are often strewn about, and I've been known to take down phone numbers in the dust on the dresser. But most of the time, it's clean enough, even if "clean enough" means it doesn't look like anything vegetable based recently exploded in it. My reasons for reforming are partly selfish: I spend most of my day in my home, and if it feels too messy or cluttered, I want to retreat and watch bad TV instead of being productive.

Buh-bye, dust bunnies

While I want our home to look "lived-in," I don't want "by a family of muskrats" to get added to that. Like it or not, there are certain tasks we all have to stay on top of to keep from being cast on *Hoarders*. Still, I can think of a lot of things I'd rather do than polish the kitchen cabinets. This chapter is not intended to put pressure on the housekeeping front. Instead, it will help you figure out which tasks you'll want to do because they help you feel free and functional instead of overwhelmed. We'll also talk about how to make housecleaning less of a hated chore for the whole family. Whether you or your spouse is the resident neat freak, I'm guessing that one of you could use a few cleaning tips to help make everyone a little saner.

Understanding how you approach (or avoid) keeping your home in order makes it easier to master the mess (unless you're already a housekeeping maven, in which case, kick your feet up for today!). A good first step is to identify your triggers—what drives you insane? Shoes kicked off by the door or papers on

What really drives you insane? Shoes kicked off by the door? Papers on the dining room table?

the dining room table? We all have things that get under our skin, making the house feel out of control. Taking care of your biggest crazy-makers (before they get to the point of actually driving you crazy) sets a much calmer and more productive tone, and may inspire you to put something else in order, too.

The quiz on page 86 will help you assess whether you struggle more with clutter or dirt, or if both make you freak out.

"I had to increase my tolerance of a mess. We have toy pick-up times throughout the day: before meals, leaving, nap time, bath time, and guests. At first, cleaning was a game. When that got old for our daughter, we said, 'You're too little to clean up yourself,' and the pick-up happened magically!" -*Momma*

Q/A

Some of us like things nice and orderly. Others of us wouldn't know a sponge unless his last name was SquarePants. Which best describes you?

1 *You have 15 minutes to clean the kitchen, so you:*
   a. Mop the floors, clean out the microwave, scour the sink.
   b. Wipe the crumbs off the counters and line up the canisters in size order.
   c. Take one look at the mound of dishes in the sink and decide to eat out tonight.
   d. Panic. Fifteen minutes? That's not enough time to clean!

2 *What's most likely to cover your bathroom countertops?*
   a. Depends if it's before or after the morning's quick wipe.
   b. A pretty assortment of bottles, tubes, and jars.
   c. A sticky assortment of bottles, tubes, and jars.
   d. Nothing except the gleaming sunlight streaming in from the sparkling windows.

3 *What does "cleaning the house" mean to you?*
   a. Scrubbing, mopping, dusting, disinfecting.
   b. Picking up toys, putting things away, and generally clearing clutter.
   c. It means you're about to be invited to join Abraham Lincoln and a large, talking hedgehog for a volleyball game, because, hello, dream on!
   d. A six-hour epic that involves multiple gadgets and specialty cleaners.

4 *Which of the following are you most likely to say?*
   a. "Where is that smell coming from?"
   b. "Where did this pile of stuff come from?"
   c. "Is that smell coming from that pile of stuff?"
   d. "I can't smell the lemon furniture polish. Time to clean!"

5 *How is your relationship with stuff?*
   a. I wish I had less of it and I try to spend money on only what I need, but I feel like I can't get it under control.
   b. There's probably too much stuff in our home, but everything is always where it belongs.
   c. I once lost a child in a pile of knickknacks. Good thing I could spot her red hair!
   d. There are Tibetan monks who have more worldly possessions than I do.

Quiz key

Mostly A's: Clean Carrie
Your floors may be clean enough to eat off of, but you can't always find the kitchen table.

Mostly B's: Tidy Tracy
You don't care if those picture frames are dusty as long as they're lined up in a nice neat row!

Mostly C's: Hot-Mess Heather
You're pretty sure (okay, positive) you were born without the house-cleaning gene.

Mostly D's: Perfectionist Patty
You dare anyone to try the white-glove test in your house. In fact, you can lend them the freshly laundered glove.

Clean up

If dust gets you down, a little cleaning can be a huge boost in your mood. I know it can be hard to do something like clean our homes because we "should"—we know we should. Case in point: We should floss our teeth twice a day. The motivating trick is to do it because the result makes you happier. To help you, I've gathered some techniques that I've found helpful. To make the cut, they had to fit easily into everyday life, be efficient, and (I hope) give your mood a boost. Pick an idea and see what happens. My guess is it will become a habit, you'll feel good, and you'll be ready to tackle another one.

Stay in motion. It's easier to clean in short but frequent intervals than to try to find a solid hour (and then face down a house that looks like a science project). Face it: The minute you settle down on the sofa to watch *Ellen,* it's over. Set a goal for how you'd like the living room to look before you veg.

Exploit multitasking. You can wipe down the fridge fingerprints while your kids finish breakfast, and quiz them on their spelling words while you wipe the counters (and while they put new fingerprints on the fridge).

Dial it in. Try taking on a much-avoided task while you make a phone call. It's amazing how much more bearable it is to tackle the dirt while you're also gabbing with a friend. Invest in a headset and you can migrate between wiping noses, sweeping, and swishing cleaner around the toilet bowl. If you're not feeling chatty, use that headset to turn up the tunes!

Let it all come out in the wash. Unless you're dealing with delicates or very dark, new clothing that is likely to run, you don't need to be a stickler for separating laundry.

Wipe down sinks once a day. Seeing a clean sink all 188 times each day that you wash your hands is a quick pick-me-up. Keep cleaning supplies in the kitchen and bathroom. Then

Trash it

Sometimes it can be hard to accept that the stuff that surrounds us may belong somewhere else. Less stuff, though, may be the path to peace! Items that are useless, too expensive to fix, or outdated are best abandoned.

Trash (or recycle) these now:

1 Stacks of paper related to events and parties that have already happened.

2 Worn toothbrushes or combs that are missing their teeth.

3 Out-of-date food—yes, even that fancy mango-thyme chutney from the gift basket they gave you at work a few years ago.

4 Socks with no mate.

5 Expired coupons.

Donate it

Other items, while not useless, don't feel good to have around. If it's hard to let go of things because of sentiment or because they're "still good," remember that, by giving them away, you are letting someone else enjoy them.

Pack these up in a "donate" box:

1 Clothes that don't fit, or that never leave the closet because they don't make you feel good.

2 Gifts you never liked.

3 Stuffed animals (or other remnants of your tween's babyhood) that now live on the closet shelf.

4 Craft projects that you started but are now collecting dust.

5 The smoothie maker you bought before you realized it serves the same function as the blender you already had, as well as any other neglected household tools.

you can easily wipe any surface visibly in need of attention, like when you see a pee puddle. (With four boys, this happens about six times a day!) If you give the bathroom a few minutes of attention daily, you'll never again have to don hazmat gear before tackling the job.

Just do it. If you think to yourself, "This weekend I've got to dust those lamp shades," chances are, plenty of things will come up between now and then to bump 'em off the agenda. What if you grabbed a dust cloth and took care of it right now? (Also see the "two-minute rule" on page 103 for inspiration.)

Conquer clutter

Caveat: I'm not going to tell you to get rid of your stuff. We all have certain things—magazines, special knickknacks, or college memorabilia—that we enjoy and, yes, make us feel happier. I encourage you to streamline and tidy up the things you love so that you can enjoy them and to be thoughtful about adding to your collections.

If you're like me, being surrounded by clutter can be a mood killer. The good news? Organizing things that you see and use daily can be an easy fix. It doesn't take any longer to hang your keys on a hook than it does to toss them on the table—or was it in your purse, which is missing too? The first option helps keep the house neat; the other adds to the mess (and will have you launching a *CSI*-type search when you're already ten minutes late dropping your kids off at school).

Establish a coming-home routine. If your house is a disaster and you don't know where to start, this can be an easy first step. Your "I'm home" routine could consist of hanging up coats (consider a row of child-height hooks near the entryway), lining up shoes by the door, and putting your purse (with your keys in it), backpacks, lunch boxes, etc. in designated spots. Work with your kids to make it a habit every time you get home, and soon everyone will do it automatically.

Keep a basket in every room. Throw in stuff that belongs in another area of the house. Enlist your kids to make deliveries and encourage them to fetch their own wayward belongings.

Break up with your baggage. If you're drowning in stuff, go through your house with a large trash bag and try to fill it with things to donate to a thrift store. When it's full, put it in the car to drop off. Do this weekly until things feel more under control. Then always keep a "donate" bag handy.

Be careful about what you allow into the house. If grocery shopping at big-box stores means you come home with bags of nongroceries you didn't exactly need but couldn't quite pass up, you didn't save any money. Accept offers of toys or sports equipment only if you or the kids will really use them—same for that shiny pasta machine your friend says she never has time to crank up. Will you, either, when a box of lasagna costs a dollar on sale? Use your noodle!

Delay a couple of days before buying. If something catches your eye, try waiting, and be wary of the lure of a sale! If that teal lambswool cardigan is meant to be yours, it'll probably still be there in a few days. The exception: Buy immediately any jeans that make your butt look smaller.

Be ruthless about tossing school papers. Yes, even that cotton-ball bunny your three-year-old made in preschool. Keep some special pieces that remind you of your child, like his first "family portrait" that included "Pink Bear," or snap photos before you recycle them. But you aren't obligated to hold on to every marshmallow statue for the rest of your life.

Don't go it alone. Maintaining your house yourself might be satisfying to you. If doing it makes you happy, that's wonderful. It's more likely, though, that trying to go solo will build resentment that's counterproductive to happiness. If it's within your means, consider hiring a housecleaner. It's cheaper than a marriage counselor. If you do have someone clean your house, it's a good idea to tidy up ahead of time so nothing gets misplaced, but try not to go overboard; remember you're paying that person to do the heavy lifting.

Working together

Everyone who lives in the house—spouse, kids, that friend of your son's who's always there—can, and should, pitch in. Chores teach kids about giving back, helping out, and being part of a team. Even tots can put their dirty clothes in a hamper and silverware on the table. The more you involve family members in caring for the house, the more you'll set the stage for happy family life, which is the end goal.

If you have young children, save yourself from sniffing out sour milk by training them—from the time they can walk—to put dirty sippy cups in the sink. Older kids can take on chores like vacuuming, doing laundry, and taking out the trash. When

Pulling back smooth covers instead of climbing into a rumpled mess of sheets makes me happier.

you hand chores off to your kids, it's reasonable to expect them to do a decent job, but they probably won't deliver perfection. However, learning how to be competent around the house is a life skill that may keep them from being a guest on *Divorce Court* in 2038. Remember the "triggers" we talked about earlier? I recommend you, not your kids, take care of those. If it's important to you that your counters are sparkling, it's probably better to do it yourself and be happy with the results.

If you have a spouse, dividing household chores is often a huge hot-button issue. For instance, a spouse working outside the house might not understand why a stay-at-home parent can't do all the housework and childcare—or even understand the scope of what that involves (I do!). Resolving this issue is about more than a clean house: It's about how well you communicate, show respect for each other, and work as partners. How much of the housework each of you takes on will depend on your family's circumstances, including the amount of work you each do outside the home, how much your kids can help out, and your budget for outside help. In chapter 10, we'll discuss how to renegotiate if you feel like you're the one always left holding the dishrag.

Pillow talk

I used to roll out of bed, look at the tangled sheets and blankets, and think, "Eh, what's the difference? I'm going to mess it up again tonight." But every time I walked into my bedroom, the sight of that unmade bed made me feel like crawling back into it. So one day, I decided to start making my bed to see if it made a difference in my mood.

It took a couple of weeks to get into the habit of making my bed every day, but soon I found myself looking forward to the task. It feels like tearing out a fresh sheet of notebook paper—clean, crisp, and full of possibility. Now, no matter how the rest of the house looks, my bedroom is a pleasant retreat. And when I turn in for the night, it's satisfying to pull back smooth covers instead of climbing into a rumpled mess of sheets. It makes me happier.

Everybody has a different tolerance level for mess. Your house might always be a bit less organized than your best friend's, and that's fine. The point is not to enter into a model-house competition with other mothers but to figure out how clean and neat you need your surroundings to be in order for you to feel good in them. So get your family on board and start somewhere, preferably with whatever mess or disorder that bugs you the most. Soon you'll figure out what housekeeping tasks have the most impact on your mood with the least amount of effort. Once you make doing those a habit, you'll enjoy your home sweet home even more.

(easy jump start)

Put away ten items, or enlist whatever kids are old enough, set a timer for ten minutes, and pick up until the bell rings.

8

have a plan

I know, I know. I spent an entire chapter saying go with the flow. Now I'm telling you another secret to being a happier mother: Have a plan. Make up my mind already, right? Rest assured, however, I'm not going to suggest you map out every hour of your day, or every year of the next five. When I say, "Have a plan," it's in the loosest of senses.

After all, you can't plot out every aspect of your life (think back to your childhood schemes—are you now married to one of the New Kids on the Block?). But trust me, plans can help you feel happier. Why? It's not because the process of planning is fun—though it can be, like the anticipation when you're planning a special event or trip. It's because when you have a good idea of where you're going and how you more or less expect to get there, you feel more in control of your life. With more control comes more confidence, and that confidence translates into less worry and more happiness.

Learning how to manage your time from day to day is as important as planning for the long term, and it has a more immediate effect on your mood. The more efficiently you use the hours and minutes (even seconds!) you've got, the more time you'll have for doing the things you want to do (like watching the Food Network) rather than only the things you have to do (like actually cooking).

Now if you're starting to panic, thinking, "Planning's not my thing!" no worries. Part of figuring out the best way to get a hold of your time today (the groceries) and the future (saving for retirement) is to understand your natural tendencies. Most of us are stronger at either envisioning the big picture or thinking through the finer details. Both are important, and maybe both are on your mind.

Find your best way to plan

It's easier to plan if you know your planning strengths and can compensate for any weaker spots. Taking the quiz on page 98 will help you determine which way you lean on the planning spectrum. Do you dream big, but sometimes fall short on implementation? Or do your family and friends rely on you to make sure all the i's are dotted and t's are crossed?

Your tendencies may shift depending on context. You may be up to speed on every detail at work but along for the (slightly chaotic) ride at home—or vice versa! I used to describe myself as "detail oriented." But I came to realize that I was good only

You might be surprised at how much happier planning can make your day-to-day life.

at specific kinds of detail, like noticing typos in the school newsletter. (Doesn't anyone proofread those things?)

When doing long- or short-term planning, try to keep in mind your tendencies and the things you most frequently overlook. If no detail escapes your notice (and believe me, I envy you), push yourself to think bigger (buy a boat!). If the big picture is more your scene, try to follow through in more detail (research, realize a boat costs more than your house, then join a monthly sailing club instead).

If you prefer to wing it and avoid planning altogether, consider giving it a shot. You might be surprised at how much happier it can make your day-to-day life.

Q/A

What's your plan-ahead style?

When looking to the future, are you a big-picture person, or do you just have the details covered?

1 *Which of these scenarios is most likely to happen to you?*
   a. The cable goes out, so you call customer service, which you put on speed dial the first time it happened.
   b. The cable goes out, so you spend the next hour sifting through the stack of mail on the kitchen counter to see if you forgot to pay the bill. Again.
   c. The cable goes out, so you improvise with Netflix for the kids while looking up the customer-service number. Or you just head to the library.

2 *When you think about where you'll be living in ten years, you:*
   a. Come up blank. There's so much going on now (three kids, a spouse, an au pair, a dog, and a full-time job all color-coded in your calendar), it's hard to think about next year, much less the rest of your life.
   b. Feel excited. You've got so many big plans for what you'll do in the future—as soon as you're not doling out M&Ms for potty-training progress.
   c. Have a pretty good idea of where you'd like to be, but you still keep in mind that any number of details (like where your child applies to college or how well your mutual funds perform) could end up changing the endgame.

3 *Your minivan blows a tire on the highway. You're:*
   a. Prepared. You're armed with an AAA card and a jack in the trunk, and you know how to use them.
   b. Nervous. Taking the kids on a road trip seemed like a good idea when you left. Now you aren't sure you have a spare. And where is the user's manual?
   c. Annoyed, but calm. Sure, you might not have the tow truck driver's number stashed in the glove compartment, but you at least have a charged-up cell phone.

4   *It's time to pick a preschool for your three-year-old. How does the process go?*
   a. You have a spreadsheet full of all available data (teacher-child ratio, test scores, number of excellence awards, average number of years' experience per teacher) from a dozen contenders within a two-mile radius.
   b. The little building down the street gets your vote. Sure, you don't know what the kids do all day or how much it costs, but look at the adorable murals of smiling children on the walls!
   c. You've done your homework and have a pretty good idea which programs align best with your child's needs. Now it's time to consider logistics like class times, but you won't sweat little details—like which school churns out a slightly higher rate of future high school valedictorians.

5   *Which of the following is more likely to happen to you?*
   a. You spend hours clipping coupons from a half-dozen stores, then realize you ended up spending an extra hour (and a couple of bucks' worth of gas) to save thirty-five cents on a can of tomato paste.
   b. You are so proud that you remembered to bring eco-friendly bags to the grocery store that you forget what you came to buy.
   c. You forgo the coupons, but remember your shopping list and do your best to choose on-sale stuff.

Quiz key

Mostly A's: The Detail Dominatrix

Appointments? On 'em! Paperwork? No prob. But if somebody asks you where you see yourself in five years, you're as fuzzy as a Beanie Baby. It's a huge asset to have an organized, efficient mom in the house. But every so often, try to look up from your daily to-do list and month-at-a-glance calendar, and take some time to dream, plan, and save for the future.

Mostly B's: The Heroine of the Horizon

You've got your eyes on the prize in the more or less middle-distance—that cool kiddie party you'll be throwing next month, the fab second career you'll eventually embark on once the kids are driving themselves. It's the small stuff that continues to trip you up; you wish Hallmark would come out with a "Sorry I double-booked playdates" card.

Mostly C's: The Empress of Equilibrium

Maybe you misplaced your child's birth certificate, but you gave yourself plenty of time to order a new one before the sleep-away camp registration form was due. You may not have your life planned out by nanosecond in an Excel spreadsheet, but you manage to keep things pretty well on track.

Were you surprised by what you learned about yourself taking the quiz? It's easy to hang on to a skewed view of our strengths. Most of the time, it turns out, I'm big on ideas, not so strong on implementation. Throwing five kids in the minivan to head to the lake for the day comes easily. Remembering to take the diaper bag, though, is more likely to be an issue. You could be the opposite, more comfortable with a comprehensive plan in hand before you strike out—that is, if you ever get out the door! Whatever your natural planning style, it's important to both work with your strengths and compensate for your blind spots. I know some of you will resist the idea that efficiency equals happiness, but go with it for a second: It really works!

Doing it day by day

By now you get where I'm going: Those of us more inclined to wing it might benefit from imposing a wee bit more structure on our lives. Think how much happier your kids are when they know what to expect, day by day, possibly even hour by hour. I've found that once my kids get in a habit—whether it's "no video games until after dinner" or "Cocoa Krispies are not part of a complete breakfast" (except maybe on Saturdays)—they don't fight it. Exceptions have to be made sometimes (see chapter 6 for more on being flexible), but if things constantly change, my kids get the idea that everything is up for debate.

If you're still resisting the idea of orchestrating your days too much, start with a list of the things that make up your average day, from waking up to lights out. Now, try to figure out when to do all your gotta-dos, working around anything that's fixed.

[**did you know**]

More than half of moms say the biggest problem with their schedules is not having any time for themselves. Consider marking some personal time on the calendar! Almost a third of moms would like to cut back on multitasking, and the other 16 percent want relief from crazy-busy mornings.
-Parenting.com

A morning slice of peanut butter toast and cup of tea go on my list of nonnegotiables.

Try not to neglect your needs and wants (for more about taking care of yourself, see chapter 9). For me, a morning slice of peanut butter toast and cup of tea go on this list of nonnegotiables. Reading the paper might be your don't-bug-mom-right-now time. Using this information, you can create an informal "map" of your days. This map will come in handy later, when we discuss carving out time for your interests and sharing responsibility with Dad (see pages 116 and 126).

Take a few things into consideration as you go: When are your energy levels highest? That might be the time of day that's ideal to hit the park, where you know you'll be pushing your preschooler on the swing for an hour at least. Choose the window when you feel most mentally sharp to pay bills or catch up on work you brought home from the office. When does everyone—including you—get cranky and slump? Perhaps you could pencil in some quiet time for then, when you lower the lights and read something you'll all find soothing (for your sake, nothing with purple dinosaurs, and for the kids' sake, no homilies on the virtues of eating veggies).

If you find that one activity always seems like a huge chore, it may be the time of day you tackle it that's to blame. I realized a few years ago that bursting into tears while helping my son with his math homework was a bit of an overreaction (but not by much—there's a reason trigonometry and tragedy share so many of the same letters). But we were doing it right before bedtime, when my mental and emotional reserves were tapped like a Vermont maple in March. Moving homework help to the late afternoon made me feel saner. Experiment until you get into a daily cadence that feels right, and then try to repeat it, day after day, until everyone in the house gets used to it.

Every so often, your rhythm will need a reboot: Your toddler drops a nap, soccer season starts, or you go on vacation and return jet-lagged. In the summer, bedtime at our house turns into a whining free-for-all, and I'm not even sure if everyone actually eats breakfast. But that's okay. I can get it on track again by reviving the elements of our routine, one at a time. And when we're back to knowing what to expect, the entire household feels calmer and happier.

Get it done

Of course, a daily rhythm will be more satisfying if it includes actually checking some things off your to-do list instead of spending an entire day trying to unload the dishwasher. Take notes from the business world and time-management gurus; what they know can be applied both in the workplace and at home, as long as you allow for emergencies, like a frantic trip to the vet when your dog eats a stash of Barbie shoes.

David Allen offers excellent time-management advice in his best-selling book, *Getting Things Done*. (My editor Elizabeth swears that reading it changed her life.) Her favorite takeaway is the two-minute rule: If you come across something that takes less than two minutes, do it right away. You'll feel satisfied and be relieved not to think about it again. A side effect: Following

You don't need the latest, greatest digital organizing app, but you do need to figure out a system that works for you.

this rule is an amazing clutter buster. Putting folded laundry away in drawers takes only seconds longer than plopping it on top of your dresser, ditto for taking the recycling eight more steps to the bin rather than leaving it on the counter.

Another key piece of advice: If you ever feel overwhelmed or stuck, simply ask, "What is the next step?" Keep each step specific and manageable. For example, if your child's birthday is coming up, start by buying invitations rather than trying to plan the whole shindig start to finish.

Managing your life

With countless to-dos and calendar items, it's impossible to store all the details in your already overstuffed head. And if you try, you'll constantly be stressed and sure you're forgetting something but never quite knowing what. You don't need the latest, greatest digital organizing app, nor do you need random sticky notes cluttering the door of your fridge. What you do need is to figure out what kind of system works for you.

The super-organized and the computer-system-savvy among you might scoff at what I do to stay sort of on track. Aside from the month-at-a-view calendar, on which I note appointments

Mommy MacGyver kit

No matter how well you plan, life won't always go according to, well, plan. A first-aid kit is great, but how about on-the-go emergency gear to tuck in your purse or stash in your car?

I know you have your cell phone handy, but add to your purse:

- A clean cloth hanky. It's not just for noses. Tie it around a scraped knee until you can find a Band Aid. Mop sweat off your neck. Wrap up the extra muffin to take home.

- Baby wipes and a plastic bag. With these two items, you can clean up almost anything. Use the wipes to dab at a messy patch, and hide anything you can't deal with immediately in the bag. Then tie it closed—voilà!

- Emergency snack. Satisfy a hungry child—or parent.

- Safety pins. You never know when somebody will have a broken zipper. As a bonus, they'll help you make a superhero cape out of any blanket or towel.

Keep these in your car (along with the spare tire and jack):

- GPS. This handy device will get you back on track quick.

- Paper towels, a blanket, and a towel. These staples come in handy for cleaning, cuddling, or covering the dirty backseats left over from mud-pie-day last weekend.

- Change of clothes—for you. If you have a young child, you probably carry backup clothes for her. Keep a set for yourself, too. (No matter your kid's age, always take a change of clothes on a plane.)

and deadlines, I jot daily to-dos and random thoughts in a plain old notebook that's usually in sight. It's got that day's appointments, tasks, and reminders (such as "use the chicken breasts before Wednesday"; "throw chicken breasts away by Friday if not used"; "investigate strange smell in refrigerator no later than Sunday"). I make my list on Sunday nights, and every evening I go through the list, cross off what's done, then flip the page and start a new list for the next day—a mix of whatever's left over and anything new that comes up.

If you have a job with meetings and deadlines, or if you and your spouse split the running-around-with-kids, you probably need something beefier. One friend uses Internet-based software that color codes to-dos and calendars for her, her husband, and her son, and it sends e-mail and text message reminders. She can "invite" her husband to events, such as a niece's wedding, and put off discussing whether he has to go.

You'll know it's the right planning system when you use it instead of avoiding it.

The downside is that you can just as easily make a mistake digitally as you can on paper, and the resulting confusion is the same. Many people do fine without digital options.

No matter how great it seems, any system is only effective if it works. If you're naturally detail oriented you may thrive using a super-detailed organizing system, and if you're very visual you may prefer one that is always in sight. The most important thing is to find something that works for you. You'll know it's right when you use it instead of avoiding it.

Family planning
Another helpful planning tool is a family mission statement, or at least a discussion about your values and goals. Yes, it sounds cheesy. No, you don't have to share it with anyone else.

"Don't expect to have
the entire house cleaned
and organized every day;
it won't happen. The
kitchen and laundry were
my daily must-get-done
chores, and beyond that
I would pick one thing to
get done each day during
nap time." -RIMommy

The purpose of a mission statement is to capture your family's top-level objectives based on your shared priorities. Once you're committed to common goals, you can start filling in concrete steps to make each one a reality. Be specific and write the tasks on the calendar. For example, if one goal is to eat together more often, reserve Friday nights for a weekly pizza dinner.

If you decide to commit to a bigger project, make a list of phases and deadlines. For example, your larger objective is "spend time outdoors," and the whole family wants to run a 5K together. Go online and research nearby family-friendly races. Register. Get proper gear for everyone. Start a training program. And celebrate together after crossing the finish line.

On deadline-oriented goals, you can also work backward. Say you want to take a Disney vacation before your youngest child starts kindergarten next fall. How much money will you need to save by that time? What other details will you need to tackle, such as arranging time off from work and searching for

First, there's the problem of having only 24 hours in a day. And then some change will throw everything off.

discounted tickets? Try sprinkling the tasks over the next several months (or however much time you have) in your calendar.

Changing your tune

With everything that moms have to juggle, plans will never go perfectly all (or maybe even most) of the time. First, there's the little problem of having only 24 hours in a day, when you're pretty sure everything on your should-do (much less want-to-do) list adds up to at least 26. And when you've finally settled into a reliable routine, chances are good that something will change—your daughter quits ballet in favor of a hip-hop class on a different day, which means a new set of carpool specs—to throw everything off.

If you're already feeling overwhelmed and disorganized, reading this chapter may make you want to curl up in a ball, preferably with a blankie and Binky close by. But take heart: A few small, easy steps are really all you need to start inching toward your goals for today and the long term. (And hint: One big goal is you, but happier!)

Remember the don't-do list? See page 33. If you haven't already, make one now. It'll help you weed out what you don't want to do so you can focus on what you do.

Dedicate five minutes to planning. Get up earlier than the kids if you have to, or take time before you go to sleep, and dedicate five quiet minutes to looking over your calendar, listing your to-dos, and preparing for the coming day.

Think of one thing that would make your life easier. Do that first. For instance, you might intend to make a pantry checklist but forget until you get home from the grocery store and realize you have ten cans of red beans and no toilet paper.

The payoff

By taking a moment to make a plan and learning to manage your overall time even a little bit better, you're doing yourself a favor. In the face of one of life's many surprises ("Mom! I need to recreate the Mayan calendar on poster board by tomorrow!"), you'll feel prepared and even—dare I say it?— calm. And when an unavoidable emergency, like a flat tire or a fever, strikes, you'll feel less panicked knowing you have wiggle room on your calendar so that you can save the day.

I'm not going to lie to you: Planning will never be foolproof when kids are involved. Ease into planning by thinking about whether you're better at seeing the big picture or filling in the details, and play to your strengths. Either way, having a general direction will make life less stressful. Plus, imagine how great it will feel when a day (it will come!) *does* go according to plan.

(**easy jump start**)

On Sunday night, gather the whole family and go over the week's schedule. Also put in the calendar anything that *must* be done this week, like buying a present before the party on Friday.

9

look out for #1

I've always loved to read. As a child, I'd head to bed with a story in hand and usually finish it before lights out. (If I didn't, I'd keep reading under the sheets with a flashlight.) In high school, I stealthily read under my desk. My fascination with fiction stayed with me as I graduated from *Are You There God? It's Me, Margaret* to Margaret Atwood. I read through meals. I read on the bus and in the bathroom. I clocked the equivalent of a full-time job each week, reading for the love of it.

When I had children, and free time vanished, reading with purpose replaced reading for pleasure. I brushed up on birth methods and breastfeeding, child development and discipline. I read so many parenting books that I turned into a walking encyclopedia of all things kids-related, from Arrowroot biscuits to Zithromax. Then one day, I had a horrifying realization: I hadn't read a novel in two years. Two years! Me, who had devoted so much of my life to reading fiction! How could such a huge part of who I was get shelved (pardon the book pun)? True, my kids were my life's passion now—but another huge source of happiness had been pushed right out of the picture.

Has something like this happened to you? Maybe you used to be a pop music junkie, but now "Gaga" brings to mind a toddler in a bubble bath, not an avant-garde artiste wearing a dress made from bubbles. Or you used to work out daily, but these days the only elliptical device you employ is when you say, "And the magic word is . . ."

Being a mom requires sacrifices. But that doesn't mean we should abandon all of our own interests and ambitions. Think back to how you spent your free time before you became a mom and what you imagined you'd be doing in the future. Did you go to art gallery openings and drink the free Chardonnay? Bike 20 miles every Saturday? Imagine you'd be the first female president, but now can't gather up the energy to run for president of the PTA? How many prebaby pastimes and dreams survived your journey to motherhood? Of course, what we want changes as we get older and have kids—it's only natural. But there's no virtue (and no happy-mom potential!) in putting your hobbies and passions on permanent hold.

Bottom line: What you want to do is important and deserves attention. If you can never find a spare moment for it, can't summon up support from family and friends, or feel guilty every time you focus on yourself, you need help looking out for number one, my next secret to being a happier mom. Take the quiz on page 112 to find out what's standing in your way. Then come back here for some tips on how to make it happen.

Be a little selfish

Nod if you've ever had a night like this: You plan all day for some "me" time—a nice long walk at sunset. Then dusk approaches and the dishes call to you from the sink, and they aren't saying, "Take a nice walk." They're saying, "Where's the Palmolive?" Your husband, meanwhile, looks tired on the sofa (bless men for their ability to look pitiful while lounging on a sofa), and your kids really need somebody to play Chutes and Ladders with them, and soon you're talking yourself out of going on your walk after all. This is a common mom choice. But it's also usually the wrong choice. Yep, you heard it here first: Being selfish can be good. Very, very good.

Take the quiz on page 112

{ mom to mom }

"I am willing to give up many things to make sure my baby will have a good life, but horseback riding will not be one of those things! It may be on the back burner temporarily, but I will find time for riding as soon as I can. I have always loved horses, and I'm hoping that my daughter will learn to love riding too! I'd love to share it with her someday." -JWills

Q/A

What's holding you back, Mama?

Is something standing in the way of doing your own thing? To identify common obstacles, choose the statements you most identify with.

a   *I want to go to yoga class, but I feel like I should be the one who helps my son with his homework every night.*

b   *Between caring for the kids, cleaning, volunteering for the PTA, work, and spending time with my spouse, I'm lucky if I have time to shave both legs, let alone take up crocheting again.*

c   *I dream about going back to college, but I don't have anyone to watch the kids while I'm in class.*

d   *Every morning I wake up intending to work out. Next thing I know it's 9 PM and I'm watching* The Biggest Loser *while eating salt-and-vinegar chips. Where did the day go?*

e   *Last time I mentioned wanting to start a business, my husband said he'd like to become the next Old Spice man, but he doesn't see either of these things happening anytime soon.*

f   *I'd like to join the gym, but there's only so much room in the budget. I'm scared my three-year-old will squander his artistic potential if he has to give up his Mini Monet class.*

Quiz key

If you chose A or F: Let go of your guilt

Your kids wear UGGs while you settle for a wardrobe that's ugh, since there's only so much bread for threads. By the time you finally sit down to dinner, after making sure everyone else has what they need on their plate, your food is lukewarm and about as appetizing as a jar of strained peas. You've gotten the idea that your children come first always, even if that means there's nothing left for you. You might be an expert at hiding zucchini in your kids' spaghetti and meatballs, but you still haven't hit on the right recipe for personal happiness.

If you chose B or D: Make—or take—your time

Your dream list is a mile long, but you could count your "free" minutes on one hand. Whether you aspire to write the Great American Novel or make it through one of Oprah's Book Club titles before you've forgotten what happened in the first chapter, carving out time for yourself is your biggest challenge.

If you chose C or E: Hang out a "help wanted" sign

You're short on supporters, and you need them. Tell hubby to stop being so negative, and then start assembling the troops—whoever is willing to do stuff like keep your kids from climbing on the keys as you're practicing piano, or cheer you on as you finish your first half marathon.

Chances are good you chose answers from more than one category. Maybe even all three. Read on to find out how to invest in yourself, no matter what obstacles get in your way.

It can be hard to embrace being a little selfish. The first step is getting to the point where you feel good about looking out for yourself: If you're wracked with guilt, it's hard to enjoy going out to the movies with some friends.

It's time for a little rationalization, ladies. First of all, consider that when you leave the kids with someone else, you're giving them both a gift: special time together. Like you relish your alone time with your kids, they deserve to have that same experience with Dad, Grandma, Grandpa, and other people close to them. Now do the math. If you're feeling guilty about going to see the opera downtown, think: What percentage is that of your child's life? Not much! It's also essential that kids learn to entertain themselves, and the older your child gets, the more he'll want to spend time with his friends or alone.

You're also setting a good example. By putting "me" time on the priority list—whether it's through exercise and eating well or spending hours painting, knitting, or, well, reading—your kids will learn to see you as a whole person, not just that woman who packs heart-shaped sandwiches in their lunches. They'll learn how important it is take care of yourself, which is a value you're teaching them. And when they're parents, they'll remember your example. And as your kids grow, you can involve them more and more in your hobbies by, for instance, taking a pottery class or going geocaching together.

Beat the clock

Now that you've set aside any lingering guilt, where can you find time to do things that you personally enjoy? It's a given that most moms are insanely busy. Caring for kids and carting them around can be a full-time job, and you're frequently doing this on top of another full-time job. Single moms have it even harder, doing most of the heavy lifting alone. But keep in mind the happier you are, the happier your family will be, too. Next time you think "I wish I had time for ____," here are some ways to see where you might be able to make time.

Must-dos for a healthy you

Just as a car can't run without oil, your body can't run on PBJ crusts and a few stolen hours of sleep. Here are five must-do tasks for keeping your physical self healthy enough to be happy. They may seem obvious, but far too often, busy moms neglect doing them.

Sleep. Consider setting yourself a bedtime, or even going to sleep 10 minutes earlier than usual. Try to avoid late-night TV and do only what absolutely must be done before bed, then put the rest aside. If your child naps, take a power siesta of your own if you can swing it.

Eat. Sit down at the table for meals when you can, but stock up on healthy food you can eat with one hand. Think nuts, dried fruit, trail mix, granola bars, and bananas. Cheese sticks, squeezable yogurt, and juice boxes aren't just for kids either.

Listen to your body. You make appointments for your kids. For heaven's sake, if something hurts, leaks, itches, feels lumpy, or plain doesn't seem right, go see your doctor—now.

Wash your hands. Then wash them again. It's hard to enjoy life when you can't stop coughing. Teach your kids to wash their hands properly too and make it a no-excuses family rule. (Our fastidious six-year-old son polices at our house.)

Get moving. Have a workout routine already? Keep it up! The rest of us can sneak physical activity into our day: Walk whenever possible, park in the back of the lot, take the stairs, swing on the monkey bars. Read on for tips on adding back in a beloved activity like kickboxing or ballet.

Start by logging how you're currently spending your time in a journal. (If you made a list of typical daily activities in the previous chapter, see page 101, you can build on it by adding details.) For a few days, write down every single activity you do and when. (Yes, that includes texting your sister and checking your e-mail 5,532 times.) Once you see where your minutes go, it might become clear that some nonessential activities are eating up precious potential "me" time. Think about what you can give the heave-ho, what you can cut back on, and what you can delegate to somebody else.

Hours-long blocks of free time are likely a thing of the past, but you can do a lot with the 10- or 15-minute blocks you do have. Look at it this way: A year is going to go by whether or not you go for that run or go for drinks. How do you want to spend it?

Make a commitment

If you're having trouble getting started, simply ask yourself: What is the first step? It's usually the hardest one to get motivated to do, which means it gets easier from there! Maybe

Make a bargain that you'll simply show up to whatever it is you've been aiming to do, and take it from there.

you could call the parks department right this minute and register for that kayaking class or go online to order that book you've been dying to read. Whatever it is, you'll feel so much better about yourself even for simply getting started; you'll instantly feel happier.

After that, make a bargain with yourself that you'll show up for whatever it is you've been aiming to do, and take it from there. For instance, if you get home after commuting and would rather tuck yourself in bed with the kids than head back out to the tai chi class at the Y, remind yourself that you made a commitment (and wrote a check!). You can do almost anything for a few minutes, so decide that you'll go for the first 10 or 15, and leave if you're still too tired. Chances are an hour will go by and you'll feel great—and accomplished.

To keep the momentum going, make your activity a habit. Get an audio version of the newest biography to listen to when you're waiting in the car. Put your Tuesday cooking class in the family calendar, and go. Do your econ homework first thing Saturday morning. Yes, this takes discipline, but the more consistent you are, the easier it will be for everyone. Pretty soon, your family will probably adapt its routine around it—your partner won't schedule conflicting activities and might start taking the kids out for doughnuts (what did you think I'd say, steamed fish?), so the house is quieter while you study.

If you have trouble getting going, the problem could be fatigue (surviving on coffee and chasing down kids on Heelys does this to a person). Consider this: Energy begets energy. The more active you are and the more fun you're having, the more motivated you'll be to keep going. If you really can't get moving, see a doctor to rule out an underlying health problem, like depression or a thyroid issue, both common in women. This is especially important for new moms because of the risk of postpartum depression. (See page 115 for self-care tips.)

Enlist your mate

If you have a significant other who always looks annoyed at the thought of your leaving for the night, it's hard to feel good about going to your sci-fi book club. If his promises to hold down the fort so you can work out unravel more regularly than a Slinky, it's easy to feel resentful. A talk may be in order. Start by making sure your partner understands how important this activity is to you and how much happier you are when you have time for it. If he feels your family's schedule is too packed, look at places where you can cut back to make room for what you want to do. Consider ways you can work as a team to help make your "me" time less stressful on the family. For instance,

Five brilliant boredom busters

No way around it, raising kids comes with a whole bunch of boring. But you don't have to succumb to the tedium, and your mind doesn't have to melt. Try these picker-uppers:

1 **Flex your intellect.** While you're waiting for choir practice to let out, read a whole *New York Times* article without stopping to check your e-mail or Facebook.

2 **Take action.** If you're having a hard time getting motivated to get moving, sleep in your work-out tops until exercise becomes part of the morning routine.

3 **Learn something new.** Mastering a skill or learning something rewires your brain. Look online for tutorials, take a free trial class, or join a group for enthusiasts.

4 **Change the venue.** Try airing yourself out—eat in the backyard, read on the porch, go for a hike. Or play tourist in your own town and see it in a new light.

5 **Fake it till you make it.** If you're bored, pretend you're not. Soon your mood is likely to shift too. Acting as if something is true is a powerful way to make it a reality.

you could declare your busiest day of the week "sandwich night" and use paper plates to ease cleanup. Also consider asking whether there's an interest he wants to pursue, too, and come up with a plan where each of you gets regular "fun" time. (And don't argue with his version of fun. Super Mario Kart is a recognized leisure activity in at least 23 states, plus Italy.)

Get a little help from your friends

In chapter 5, we talked about the importance of a strong network of friends and family. But "network" isn't only a noun, it's a verb, too. You need to ask for and accept help. Here's how:

Be direct. "I want to take a college statistics class so I can apply for grad school next year. My company will cover the costs, but I need someone to watch the kids."

Make a specific request. "Would you be able to take the boys for two hours on Tuesday afternoons starting next week?"

Offer to reciprocate. "I can watch yours on Friday nights. My husband works late, and you and Dan could have a real date!"

Ask for ideas. Sometimes people can't help. Be gracious, but ask for ideas. "I understand. Is there anyone else I could ask?"

Make it happen

Are you dying to see a concert that isn't the Wiggles (though Anthony's kind of hot) or simply want to enjoy a bath before everyone else uses up the hot water? Your wishes matter. It's easy to get the idea that moms aren't supposed to think of our own needs, but taking time for ourselves does our kids and spouses a big favor. Happy moms project their happiness to the whole family. And while our kids may be the center of our world, it's too much pressure to expect them to be everything to you. So take steps to move past guilt, line up support, and spring into action. You'll feel more energetic. You'll be more fun to be around. And you'll love being a mom even more.

(**easy jump start**)

Pick one hobby you've dropped and would like to revisit, write down the first step to do it, and put it on your calendar in ink.

10

love your love life

The lowest point of my marriage involved a baby bottle. It was around 3 AM, and my husband, Jon, had been asleep for hours. I, on the other hand, had just fallen asleep about an hour before. Isaac, our second child, was about two months old and still in that eating-round-the-clock phase.

Our older son, Jacob, was two years old and came into our bedroom begging for a "baba wawa" (a bottle of water). I was in such a sleep-deprived haze, I could barely stay awake long enough to hear his pleas. He asked more and more loudly, threatening to wake up the baby, who in those days could be roused by a fly buzzing two rooms away, and was stirring in the bassinet attached to our bed. I reached over to pat his back, hoping desperately he'd stay asleep. Jacob continued to beg. "Baba wawa! Baba wawa!!!"

"Jon," I whispered. No response but the smooth sound of his snores. "Jon," I said a bit louder and more urgently. Nothing. I reached over and jiggled him with my foot. He didn't budge. "Jon!" I shouted. He snorted. I was consumed with a white-hot rage. How dare he sleep the night away while I was so tired I could barely remember my own name? How dare he snore?

With a heavy sigh, I finally heaved myself out of bed, stomped to the kitchen, prepared the "baba wawa," and came storming back. By now Jacob's pleas had turned into full-blown wails, and, of course, he'd woken Isaac. My burbling, bubbling anger boiled over, and as I passed Jon's side of the bed holding the bottle by the nipple, I gave him a "tap" on the head with the plastic end. Only I could instantly tell that I'd done more than tap. As the thwack registered through the room, he flew out of bed, holding his head and hollering. Both babies were wailing. I was crying. I could see the headlines: "Wife Assaults Husband with Baby Bottle." I felt awful. Had I really resorted to physical violence, even unintended? But I was still angry. Sure, I hadn't meant to do it, but deep down I thought that he deserved it.

Separation and reconciliation

Ten years later, I still look back at that night with a heavy heart. It was the beginning of more sorrow for us. A little more than a year later, we separated and eventually divorced. The good news: a couple years after that, we reconciled and remarried. We had more kids, and everything has been great since. (Though there are still times when I'd like to bop him over the head with something—of course, something soft.)

The memory also pains me because, though not everyone's story involves accidental baby-bottle violence, I see so many common threads in the experiences of other moms. Jon's and my low point in the bedroom didn't come out of nowhere. I was angry at him for so much in those days: for not seeing how tired and overwhelmed I was, for not stepping in to help, for not doing what I needed him to do, even though, to be honest, I wasn't really sure what that was a lot of the time. In short, I expected him to make me happy.

During the two years my husband and I were apart, I learned a lot about what really matters in a marriage and how to keep us from ever getting to the dividing line again. I realized that most of us are basically good people, paired with basically good people, who make mistakes and misunderstand each other. Kids add stress to the equation. Understanding this helps keep me on track during any rough times. Before I share what else I've learned about how to love your love life, my tenth secret to being a happy mom, take the quiz on page 124 to reflect on your relationship and where it might need some help.

Q/A

For better or worse?

Take this quiz to find out if you and your honey might benefit from some happiness triage.

1 *Your toddler is giving off a suspicious smell, and the dog is whining at the door. Can you count on your partner to jump in and help?*
   a. Without a doubt.
   b. Eventually, with some prodding.
   c. Not unless you threaten to put his BlackBerry in the goldfish tank.

2 *It's 8 PM. Miraculously, the kids went to bed without a fuss, leaving you and your partner alone—together. In half an hour, what would a bystander hear?*
   a. Rustling sheets.
   b. The TV.
   c. Snoring.

3 *Where does spending time as a couple rank in your priorities?*
   a. It's essential, like food, water, and chocolate.
   b. It's an occasional pleasure, like six hours of sleep.
   c. It's about as high on the list as polishing the dashboard of my car.

4 *After catching your kids sneaking Wii time without permission, you ban video games for a week. Your spouse:*
   a. Goes along with it, even if he thinks you're being a meanie.
   b. Lets the kids play when you aren't home. ("But don't tell Mom!")
   c. Is the last to know.

5 *How do your fights tend to end?*
   a. With a round of "I'm sorry!" "No, it was my fault!" and
   then a make-out session.
   b. It might take you a few hours . . . or days, but eventually
   you cool off, apologize, and move on.
   c. They don't. You'll still be bringing up that mean thing he
   said in a year.

Quiz key

Mostly A's: The Honeymooners
You still call each other by pet names, don't you? Either you
got together last week, or you've been taking tender care of
your relationship.

Mostly B's: Comfy and Companionable
You're coexisting peacefully, but spending time with him ranks
somewhere below watching *Mad Men* (you've been known to
blow him off for *Seinfeld,* too). Don't worry: At times, every
relationship gets off track. Our tips can help you reengage.

Mostly C's: Just Roommates
Every relationship goes through lulls, but this one barely has a
heartbeat. Don't call the coroner yet. Even seriously cooled-off
couples can reconnect if they try. Read on.

Balance the scales

If you've ever come home after a rare girls' night to find your unbathed kids running around an hour past bedtime in their spaghetti-sauce-stained clothes, this section is for you. Yes, the image of mom doing everything around the house while the husband skates by on his good looks and ability to operate the DVD player is a stereotype, but for many families, it rings distressingly true. Study after study has shown that women still do most of the household work—even when they work full-time outside of the home.

Anyone whose spouse has ever stepped over a pile of sneakers near the door on his way out can probably relate. Why do some guys seem so clueless? Try not to take the situation personally. It doesn't necessarily mean your partner is lazy or doesn't care about you. He may be willing to help out but isn't sure what you expect. Or he may have different standards than you when it comes to bedtime (Kids in bed before midnight? Score!) or clean floors (No muddy footprints? All right!).

Of course, that doesn't mean you have to play the maid—or the martyr. (Neither of which translates to a whole lotta happy!) You and your partner need a clear understanding of how much work is involved in taking care of kids and a home to negotiate the best way to split up the work. It's also good to agree on some basic definitions—say, what constitutes a clean stove or a child who doesn't look like he's escaped from a Victorian-era sweatshop.

Share the work

I've asked you in previous chapters to track what's happening, and here's another place where this "market research" will pay off. Try noting everything you both do around the house for a week, noting how long each task takes. Don't forget "unseen" labor—like scheduling haircuts, refereeing playdates, and chasing down the plumber. Also identify things that *should* get done but currently slip through the cracks, like hosing

Are moms in the mood for love?

When the editors of *Parenting* magazine surveyed more than 1,000 mothers, they got an earful about the state of moms' relationships. Here's what they found out:

- A mom's love life is the most important factor influencing her happiness!

- However, 39 percent of the moms surveyed reported being dissatisfied with their love lives.

- Only 35 percent of the women said they have a great sex life. Another 37 percent said that while their relationship is still close, they don't have sex as often as they used to; 14 percent stated that they're more like roommates than lovers; and a sad 7 percent admitted that their relationship (including the sex part) is in the dumps.

- Of the moms with one or two children, 44 percent reported that their partners often don't notice what needs to be done around the house or with the kids. The number goes up to 54 percent if the moms have three or more kids.

But don't throw up your hands and join a convent. By working on the areas where couples are most likely to run into roadblocks, you can take your relationship from flagging to fantastic. (If you'd settle for "perfectly fine," that'll work too.)

off the furnace filters. You might be surprised. Maybe your partner does more behind the scenes than you ever realized, like being the family's unpaid IT support. Seeing how much he contributes could give your spirits a lift, if you've been feeling resentful. If it turns out your hunch was right, though—you've been putting in the equivalent of a 40-hour week keeping the house up, while he loads the dishwasher every now and then—try not to throw the book at him (and then expect him to pick it up). He may be as surprised as you are by the inequality.

One way to address the situation is to pick one thing together to work on each week: For example, he could get the kids dressed for school while you make breakfast. Make sure to express your appreciation when he makes an effort (positive reinforcement isn't only for kids and dogs). Keep in mind that fairness doesn't necessarily mean a fifty-fifty split. Instead, your workload can ebb and flow depending on what else is going on in your life. What's important is that you both recognize what it takes to keep the house running, appreciate one another's contributions, and make an effort toward pulling your weight.

And whenever you feel like your situation needs some tweaking, be direct—no hinting, sighing, or beating around the

Whenever your situation needs some tweaking, be direct—no hinting, sighing, or beating around the bush.

bush. Hey, I'm guessing you chose your guy for his great sense of humor or sparkling wit, not his psychic ability. And he can't intuit that either, 'cause he's not a psychic.

Dollars and sense

Does your husband save for rainy days while you buy that cute Burberry plaid umbrella and the matching rain boots? Every person has a unique financial outlook and accompanying emotional baggage. So it's no wonder that couples fight about money. In fact, a recent study indicated that the more a couple fights about money, the more likely they are to split.

There's no way around it: Money is a loaded issue, and one that I cannot fully address in this book. Disputes often reflect your earning roles. Do you bring home more of the bacon or stay at home with the kids? Whatever your situation, you both have financial rights and responsibilities. If you're not up to speed on your household finances, I encourage you to learn the details. If you're having financial problems, start by reading up on personal finance or visiting a financial planner who can give you insight into your specific challenges.

When it comes to money and a harmonious partnership, it's more important than ever to talk and listen respectfully, especially about emotions. A financial system that you both like and will use—a shared spreadsheet, a bill-paying date, or a weekly review—can help reduce tensions. I also recommend that each of you have some spending money that you don't have to account for. That way, you can focus your combined attention on big-ticket items, like your son's braces (ouch!), rather than putting every latté under scrutiny.

Stay connected

When was the last time tangled sheets had nothing to do with a kid making a fort in your bed? For many moms, sex gets shoved way—and I mean *way*—down the to-do list, and for us, not getting much might not seem like a problem. Post-pregnancy and breastfeeding hormones can make your libido harder to locate than Waldo. And when you're tired, a roll in the hay may run a distant second to a good night's sleep. And that's okay—sometimes.

But it's a pretty safe bet that Dad doesn't feel the same way. And somewhere along the line, it's important to compromise. Embrace the quickie in the walk-in closet or get up a few minutes early and surprise your spouse with his favorite kind

"We've been married for 14½ years, and my definition of romance has changed. Now I think it's romantic when he deals with a sick and crying kid in the middle of the night, does the dishes, takes out the garbage before it is spilling out of the can, offers to cook dinner, or my favorite romantic thing: lets me sleep in on a Saturday!"
-Big-Mouth-Burgher

Will your spouse score

What are the chances your husband will get lucky tonight? Give him points for each of the following, and see if he scores a roll in the hay:

1 Says, "Thank you for making dinner."

2 Clears the table and stacks the dishwasher.

3 Sides with Mom that nine is too young to watch *Family Guy*.

4 Bathes child with mashed potatoes and Play-Doh in her hair.

5 Fields question about how babies are made that starts out, "This kid on the playground said . . ."

6 Finds a movie on demand for the two of you to watch together later.

...or strike out?

Hubby loses points on your scorecard for each of the following, so find out if he's out of luck this time and destined for the doghouse:

1 Steps over toys on way to sofa.

2 Settles into sofa with a beer and the remote.

3 Watches a preseason football game that he recorded and already knows how it ends.

4 Can't find your child's PJs, which have been in the top drawer since she was born.

5 Disappears on his tenth gotta-go-to-the-store trip.

6 Falls asleep on the sofa, snoring.

ot wake-up call. And once in a while—on a night when you'd really rather not, but he's looking kind of desperate—give him the chance to convince you.

If date night has gone the way of season tickets to the symphony, don't let anyone tell you that's a major tragedy. Sure, relationship gurus espouse the importance of regular date nights. But will those experts pay the sitter, pump the breast milk, and arrange for somebody to drive your teen to and from his school dance? No? When you don't have the time, inclination, or budget to go out for a date, think of ways you can connect without leaving the house. For example, my husband and I like to rent past seasons of TV shows and watch them together every night after the kids are in bed.

If you're lucky enough to get a night out together, think novelty, which researchers now say is the key to revving romance. To make your date into a relationship turbo-booster, enjoy new and different activities. While dinner and a movie might be a nice routine, it isn't going to ramp up those love receptors in the brain. Switch it up by ice skating, taking a ballroom dancing class together, or even trying a different restaurant—anything new and exciting that you both enjoy will help reignite sparks.

Forgive and then forget

Forgiving doesn't really count if you keep bringing up that fight from last month—you remember the one, when your husband forgot to put the dog in her crate before you left and she made wood pulp out of the sofa legs?—as ammunition. Even if you never bring the incident up again, if you let it simmer in the back of your brain, it's going to poison every interaction you have with your partner. It's hard to react reasonably to a small gaffe—like when your husband's running 15 minutes late for dinner because he lost track of time at work—when all you can think of is that time he missed dinner entirely after Happy Hour became A Very Happy Three Hours.

"We switch off babysitting another couple's kids for date nights. Everyone gets to go out once or twice a month, and it's free!"
-TMRivera

I'm not suggesting you live in denial: If there are major issues in your marriage, like addiction, adultery, abuse, or plain habitual jackass behavior, they need to be addressed not swept under the rug. But for the most part, we're all human beings who make mistakes.

Once a run-of-the-mill blunder has been addressed and apologized for, it needs to go into the mental trash bin. As tempting as it can be to keep that I'm-so-much-more-virtuous-than-you-and-here's-why hand grenade in your pocket to toss during a fight, holding on to old hurts doesn't do you or your relationship any good. It's up to you to let the past go, but if it's hard for you to move forward, choose a time when you're both calm to talk about it.

And while we're on the topic of forgiving and forgetting, here's a bit more ammo you can add to your happy-relationship arsenal: the art of apology. Have you ever found yourself digging in your heels during an argument because you know

It's amazing how disarming a simple apology can be. And the reward is way more powerful than being right.

you're right—or if you're wrong, he's even more wrong? It's amazing sometimes how disarming a simple apology can be. Yes, you'll have to swallow your pride. Yes, you'll have to give up on the idea of "winning" the fight. But the reward is way more powerful than being right. If your apology seems hollow, think about what you're apologizing for, and be genuine. If you aren't sorry for your actions or your opinion, don't fake it—you probably can, however, be sincerely sorry that the issue has become a conflict in your relationship.

Make yourself happy

One of my biggest mistakes in Marriage 1.0 was waiting for my husband to make me happy. Whatever I wanted—whether it was a social life, financial security, or a break from the kids—I expected him to "give" it to me (buying the orchestra tickets, getting the higher-paying job, taking the kids without being asked and leaving for the day). It took me a while to realize that, while Jon is a great conversationalist, good provider, and a capable dad, he doesn't always know exactly what I want and he doesn't always have to be the one to give it to me. I'm closer to my husband than anyone else in the world, but that doesn't mean he can be everything to me or vice versa.

It took me a while, but I finally learned that if I really wanted something, I had to take responsibility for getting it or at least asking for it directly, without hinting around. If I wanted to chat about eighteenth-century literature, I could join a book club. If I needed a nap, instead of yawning and hoping Jon got the hint, I could hand him the baby and go to bed.

Don't give up so fast

There is one similarity running through each of these relationship tips: the willingness to keep trying. So many marriages are hanging by a thread when there are young kids in the house, and all it takes is entertaining the idea of throwing in the burp cloth to start you down the path to separation. I do believe some couples would be better off apart, but keep this in mind: If you split up, you'll still have to figure out a way to parent alongside one another until your child is 18. And being a single parent isn't exactly a joy ride either.

We're all human, and we're all going to hurt each other's feelings from time to time. Take it from me: Willingness to forgive and a desire to stick it out even when your guy goes to the store to buy milk and comes home with everything but the milk (again!) can go a long, long way toward helping you keep the good stuff in mind. You know, the stuff like how much he loves to play with the baby, or how he always makes breakfast on Saturday before you get up. And the stronger your relationship, the happier you'll be.

(**easy jump start**)

If it's gone by the wayside, start a ritual of kissing your spouse "hello" and "good-bye."

Here's to happy endings

I had my first baby in 1997, when I was 20 years old. This was years before anyone had coined the phrase "mommy blog." I floated along pretty happily with our easygoing first son, Jacob, but adding our more rambunctious second boy, Isaac, just 22 months later, was a shock to the system. We'd moved to follow my husband's job, and I found myself spending long days with a toddler who wanted to play and an infant who didn't want to sleep. We lived in a third-floor apartment in Minnesota, hundreds of miles from friends and family. In the dead of winter. Did I mention it was *Minnesota*?

Bored and lonely, I focused my energy on a high-intensity ideal of motherhood that included converting an extra bedroom into a functional Waldorf classroom and baking my own bread. I spent almost every waking moment thinking about my children and worrying that making a wrong choice would scar them for life. You know, like accidentally serving up "juice drink" laden with red dye #5 instead of real juice.

For one miserable year, I rarely took a moment for myself. No surprise, I was exhausted, anxious, and unhappy. Plus my marriage had become icier than the weather outside. In the summer of 2000, my husband and I separated, and we divorced a little more than a year later. (Miraculously, we got back together a couple of years later and added three more kids to the family—you can read about that in chapter 10.)

My bout as a single parent jolted me off the merry-go-round of motherly misery. Worried more about putting dinner on the table than putting organic cotton on my kids' backs, I made parenting choices I would have never imagined, like sending my children to daycare and feeding them prepackaged snacks! And the kids did just fine.

As I adopted a more laid-back approach to motherhood—more like the way my own mom raised my two brothers, sister, and me—I became much happier. I actually enjoyed my kids, rather than seeing them as my personal mission in life. Of course, I still had standards, like occasionally saying "yes" to clear soda but always "no" to the brown stuff (hey, I didn't say my standards were always logical), but they were those that mattered to me, not anyone else.

Instead of parenthood being a chore, a burden, and "the hardest job in the world," I began to look at it as a relationship that changes daily. Sometimes being a mom is great, and sometimes having kids makes you tear your hair out. But overall, I'm a happy mom.

I'm an optimist. I know being a mom can be messy, but I think moms can be, and deserve to be, happy.

Mommy media has come a long way since I started having children. As moms like me found their voices online, first through forums and later blogs, we dished about colic, crying, cramping, and bodily fluids of all sorts. And it was great—mostly. Books and blogs about motherhood were heavy with words like "sanity" and "survival," and light on words like "happiness" and "enjoyment." The more I read, the more I suspected we'd gotten so "real" that we'd forgotten about the happier side of being parents.

I'm an optimist. While I know being a mom can be messy, frustrating, and plain exhausting, I think moms can be, and deserve to be, happy. That's why I started my blog, TheHappiestMom.com, in 2009. I hoped to fill the void and let moms know that it's possible to be a happy parent. I hoped that sharing my journey from crisis to contentment would inspire other moms to do the same.

It's been an exercise in self-discovery, too. I've learned what makes me tick (daily exercise and quiet time, good!) and what ticks me off (clutter on the table and my kids using their "outdoor voices" indoors, bad!). I've also heard from other moms about what makes them happy and what gets in the way. My readers and I have embarked on a quest to become more upbeat and satisfied—not only for our own sakes but for our families' as well.

My blog is a daily snapshot of my journey. As I started to identify things every mom can do to make her life a little easier, so that she can be a whole lot happier, I wanted to share these tips with a wider audience. Teaming up with the editors of *Parenting* magazine made it possible. Together we gathered the most helpful, practical advice and combined it with *Parenting*'s detailed research into moms' inner worlds and input from hundreds of thousands of moms on Parenting.com. The result is this beautiful book.

I know you're most likely crazy busy, and the last thing you need is one more looming obligation on your to-do list. ("Be happy? Sure, I'll get to that as soon as my cupboards are organized.") My hope is that *The Happiest Mom* will inspire you to try a few ideas that will streamline and de-stress your life. And if nothing else, I hope that the positive (but realistic) examples here will show you that you're not alone and that you're already doing a great job. Just knowing that, I bet you're happier already.

Meagan Francis

Write your own happy ending

Here's some space where you can dream, doodle, or jot down any "aha" notes-to-self. No worries if it ends up smudged with coffee and chocolate stains. These pages are yours, all yours.

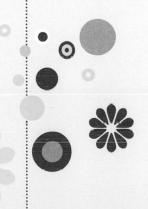

Index

Acknowledgments

First and foremost, a huge thank-you to my editor, Elizabeth Dougherty, for believing in this book and working with the talented teams at Weldon Owen and *Parenting* to make it a reality. Thank you to *Parenting's* Elizabeth Anne Shaw for her support and to Deborah Skolnik for her laugh-out-loud editing. Also, a shout-out to Angela Williams for her fantastic design.

Thanks to my writer's group. You ladies are more comfortable than a good nursing bra and twice as supportive.

Every mom needs a tribe. To the friends and family who have cheered me on, wrangled my kids so I had time to write, been happy mom role models, and made parenting a bit more fun by sharing those sweaty trips to the museum and post-doughnut meltdowns (the kids', I mean) with me, thank you.

And thanks to the mom blogging community and the Yaapsters, who have been with me since the days I yearned to be the kind of perfect mom who knits her own baby diapers out of free-range, organic yak hair. I appreciate that you stuck with me even after I switched to conventional yak hair.

Thanks to Mom and Dad, for never making parenting us seem like a burden. Even when it was.

Thank you to Jon for never making a trip to the store without bringing back something for me. And then going out again if I change my mind.

And to Jacob, Isaac, William, Owen, and Clara, for giving me five reasons to be happy every day.

Parenting

Executive Editor *Elizabeth Anne Shaw*
Senior Editor *Deborah Skolnik*

2 Park Avenue
New York, NY 10016
www.parenting.com/store

Weldon Owen Inc.

President, CEO *Terry Newell*
VP, Publisher *Roger Shaw*
Executive Editor *Elizabeth Dougherty*
Editorial Assistants *Elizabeth Clark
  and Katharine Moore*
Creative Director *Kelly Booth*
Art Director *Angela Williams*
Designer *Michel Gadwa*
Illustrator *Jeff Barfoot, Bee Things*
Production Director *Chris Hemesath*
Production Manager *Michelle Duggan*
Color Manager *Teri Bell*

415 Jackson Street
San Francisco, CA 94111
www.wopublishing.com

Parenting and Weldon Owen are
divisions of Bonnier Corporation.

Library of Congress Control Number: 2010935860

ISBN 978-1-61628-060-4

10 9 8 7 6 5 4 3
2011 2012 2013 2014

Printed by Toppan-Leefung Printing Ltd. in China.

About *Parenting* The premier U.S. magazine for moms, *Parenting* provides honest, real-world advice on raising children and the emotional support and connection mothers need to enjoy their full lives. Founded in 1987, *Parenting* has more than 2 million subscribers. It remains the cornerstone of The Parenting Group family, which includes Parenting.com and *Conceive* and *Babytalk* magazines.

About Meagan Francis A parenting author, blogger, and columnist, Meagan is also a contributor to *Parenting* magazine. She has been featured in interviews on NBC, MSNBC, and in *The New York Times*, and she blogs at TheHappiestMom.com. Her first two books are *Table for Eight* and *The Everything Health Guide to Postpartum Care*. She coauthored *One Year to an Organized Life with Baby*. Meagan has four sons and one daughter and lives with her family in Saint Joseph, Michigan.

About Christine Carter, PhD A happiness expert known for her science-based parenting advice, Christine is a sociologist at the Greater Good Science Center at the University of California, Berkeley. She is also the author of *Raising Happiness: 10 Simple Steps for More Joyful Kids and Happier Parents*. Christine offers online parenting classes at RaisingHappiness.com and serves on *Parenting*'s advisory board, the Mom Squad. Christine has two daughters and lives near San Francisco.